If My Product's So Great,

How Come I Can't Sell It?

Based on the Three Scripts Class

If My Product's So Great,
How Come I Can't Sell It?

Four Agreements for Marketers
100 Customers 100 Days

Kim Klaver
with Heidi Dulay

Kim Klaver Productions
Las Vegas, Nevada

ISBN 1-891493-11-6
Printed in the United States of America
First Printing

To the lovers out there…and especially

for

Vicki Link, who, with a three-day notice on her trailer home door in the Spring of 1994, went door to door with a box of product she borrowed from me, to gather enough customers so she could get to the first management position in her first 30 days in my group, and who, within nine months of that day, went on stage with me at the national convention as the proudest of my first three National Marketing Directors. She was given top honors by the company, NSA, and inducted into the company's Hall of Fame, because she had created and lived out her own big rags to riches story that is perhaps the best known and most admired in the history of the company.

Acknowledgments

I owe many debts to many people.

First, to my thousands of students and fans over these last eight years, who have had the courage to stay the course with their network marketing business, despite many unexpected obstacles, including the ultimate - watching their own company tank, and having to get up and find another one. Without determined, good people like you, what would the industry of direct sales and network marketing do?   And what would I do?

I am grateful to some 1500 pioneering students who have participated in the Three Scripts 100 Customers 100 Days class. Throughout the laughter and the agony of some of the script doctoring sessions, those who are using the scripts have changed the course of their businesses.   I am delighted.   Each one of you deserves huge success for having the courage to try something new and different.

I'd especially like to thank the note takers and scribes, who helped in each class take down the various versions of the scripts as they were being developed live in class. The reps include Miriam Hawley at Excel, Cheryl Henderson-Khalid, now at Shaklee, Dawn McDonald at Ideal Health, Elizabeth Yandle at Shaklee, Marjorie Rosborne at Ameriplan, Lin Young at InnerLight, Peg Lewis for seven Shaklee classes, and for the last 27 Mannatech, Mixed, and Shaklee classes, Heidi Dulay at LittleSpa.com. If I've overlooked someone, please email me at Kim@WhoWho911.com and I'll fix it.

Special thanks also to those who introduced the early classes to many others in their companies, including Jacqueline Freeman for Excel, Ray Gebauer and Carol Merlo for Mannatech, Mary Ann Cohee and Jim Hary for Integris, Cheryl Buck for Ideal Health, and Bob Ferguson and Peg Lewis for Shaklee. I'm grateful to Peg Lewis and Cheryl Buck for being excellent Teaching Assistants in the classes and Study Halls for their companies, to my stellar Training Director Vicki Link for

vii

assisting me in the Three Scripts Study Halls for mixed companies and for running the Three Scripts clinics for graduates who needed extra assistance. Many thanks also to Cheryl Buck and Elizabeth Yandle who were Script Doctors for their companies, Ideal Health and Shaklee, respectively.

I want to thank John Milton Fogg for falling in love with Three Scripts and shamelessly promoting it to his entire TGN network.

I am grateful to those who contributed to the look of this book: Gillian Riley of Phrizbie Design for the cover design and graphics, my wonderful layout editor and dear friend of 25 years Maria Hyman, and Don Miguel Ruiz, author of *Four Agreements*, from whom I borrowed the subtitle of this book and the font I chose for the whole book. Thanks also to Beth Greer for her valuable comments on early snippets of this book.

If I have missed anyone, write and let me know. I'll do my best to make updates in a timely manner – you know – in our lifetime.

Special Acknowledgment

This book would not have happened in my lifetime without the world class writing and editing hand of my dear friend of 33 years, *Dr. Heidi Dulay*. Teaching concepts and scripts is one thing when done live and over the phone, but writing about it is another matter, as I have discovered. Almost every line in the text has been improved by Heidi's perceptive mind and skillful hand.

Now, let's get to it, shall we?

Contents

Assembling Your First Date Script ~ 103

When Someone Says Yes: Scripts 1, 2 and 3 ~ 129

Should I Tell Them about the Business? ~ 162

**Fourth Agreement:
Do It Over and Over
and Over and Over and Over and Over** ~ 174

**PART TWO
100 CUSTOMERS 100 DAYS** ~ 197

The Launch ~ 199

Finding Your Audience ~ 212

Three Tips to Keeping Them Listening ~ 222

Email Signatures ~ 294

A Website for Customers ~ 310

First Foreword

This book has been brewing for many years. I was eight years old when I sold my first Christmas cards. My Dad worked for a publishing company that put out greeting cards I really liked, and he told me I'd earn 40 cents for each box I sold. We had just arrived in the U.S. from the Netherlands, and I could barely speak English, but I went from door to door through my entire neighborhood anyway, and earned more than all the kids I knew who were also doing it. The same people bought my cards every year...

This book is about doing that with any product you love. It's about getting long term, loyal, regular customers. The kind of customer who looks forward to seeing whatever new stuff your company comes out with.

Like I look forward to hearing about anything new Apple is coming out with, and I've bought a lot from them over time.

The approach, the scripts, and the tips in this book come out of decades of selling. I feel like I've made every mistake and hit every obstacle. Each time, I've picked myself up, brushed off the dust and started again, hopefully wiser than before.

The book is based on the first 45 three-day classes I gave in 2003 called "Three Scripts -- 100 Customers 100 Days". Over 1,500 direct marketers from some 47 companies attended the classes. Their reactions during the classes and the results they reported after using what they learned, inspired me to make the teachings available in this form.

The class title refers to the three main scripts a direct marketer uses when selling: the approach script (which I call the "First Date Script"), and the responses to "What is it?", "Will it work for me?", and "How much does it cost?"

The subtitle came to me one day while reading that MCI was launching a big customer campaign over the next 100 days. I thought, why don't we do that too? 100 customers in 100 days. I knew that with the right approach, the right words, and a much-loved product or service, we could do it too.

The next foreword is for networkers. If you have never been one, skip it and go to Chapter 1.

Ready?

Second Foreword
To Network Marketers

Network marketing is perhaps the only business where one has to justify going after customers.

In every other business, customers are sacred. Companies do everything they can to woo and keep them. Nordstrom, for example, has built their entire business by offering outrageously good customer service.

But, how often have you heard, especially from people at the top of your heap, that it's a waste of time to go after customers? That the money is in recruiting business builders? Hmm.

What's the story here? Why are customers at the low end of everyone's totem pole in the network marketing business?

For some it's because income from customers looks like small potatoes compared to the big money a business builder might bring. And the few people who get builders in their organizations are the ones showcased in front of the room.

These big earners are the ones who have been fortunate enough to stumble upon a business builder or two[1], who bring in a whole organization of aspiring builders. Soon there are thousands of people selling the dream to others, and everybody is buying product regularly so that they can be a "product of the product". And this rare top banana, at the top of the heap, gets a percent of most all of it. That's why the income gets so big.

Nice work if you can get it.

However, everyone who's been in the business for a year or more knows the downside: the odds of getting an entrepreneur who really does something and stays with it until, are almost as small as winning the lottery.

---

[1] None of the 70+ top bananas earning $30,000 or more per month whom I have interviewed over the years have more than four people giving them 85-95% of their income. Most have one person whose organization contributes at least half of their income. And as often as not, that key player was not sponsored directly by the top banana.

How many of you have succeeded in finding those entrepreneurs? And in keeping them? …

For years, when I was building my various network marketing businesses, I too focused on finding aspiring marketers. I used to call them "turbos" because they started with the larger volumes of product ($2,000 to $25,000), so that they could instantly achieve a higher commission level. These initial purchases gave my income a turbo boost.

So, I went after them with a vengeance, enjoying the "big money" for a good while. But I had to work 10- to 12- hour days to sustain the income because most of the turbos lasted less than three months. They'd sign up, buy the quota and were gone in a couple of months. Some would disappear in a week.

Most really weren't business builders. They were mesmerized by the financial promise of the circles on the wall and my success. They forgot that I had been working at it relentlessly for five years previously, plus, I had finally "won the lottery". I had stumbled across an extraordinary business builder within the first three months of starting my fifth network marketing business.

The starry eyed "turbos" I signed up would use the product themselves, and sit on the rest. They discovered they really didn't enjoy selling, and their initial enthusiasm disappeared in the face of the unresponsive or unexpected pukey treatment they got from their friends, family, and the general marketplace.

So, I often ended up moving the product for them, so they wouldn't be "garage qualified" or have to send it back. To speed up moving product, we started an "automatic reorder" program in our organization, so that customers could commit to using the product every month, at a preferred price.[2]

In hindsight, 97% of the people I signed up ended up being just customers. And I was getting them the hard way – by leading with the business. There are

---

[2] The company I represented liked this idea and ended up adopting that automatic reorder program company-wide. They called it the Preferred Customer Program, and today, they have tens of thousands of regular monthly customers. Many other companies have similar programs, often called "autoship."

way fewer people who sell a product than use it. Data from several large network companies show that for every 100 people who regularly order a product or service for their own use, only two or three also sell the product. Around 97 are just customers, not distributors, even though many were signed up as distributors. So, why not woo customers to begin with? It's a less stressful and more predictable way to build significant income.

At the end of the Chapter 1 "Take Off", you'll run through a little exercise that causes many of my students to gasp with delight. It demonstrates just how much income you can make from regular monthly customers. Certainly enough to provide some necessary insurance against the possibility that it might take longer than you expect to find that Ace.

Something in the bank for those rainy times…

Kim
Mill Valley, California
In the Spring of 2004

Part One

4 Agreements
3 Scripts

1

Take Off

In the last 15 years of working with direct marketers, I've met thousands of people who sell products or services because they love them. Yet they struggle with their business, and often it's been a long struggle over many years. Most tell me how a health supplement or a new service has changed their lives forever, and they cannot fathom why everyone isn't falling over themselves to buy it, if not sell it too:

*"It's a product that everybody needs. And I thought everyone would want it. Isn't everyone tired all the time? Doesn't everyone want more energy? But **when they have to spend money, boy, suddenly it's sure different!**"*

*"**It takes longer than you think.** I'm a go-getter and I thought it would be a slam-dunk. But it wasn't. I'm still getting over it. **They took away some of my self-confidence.**"*

3

*"Boy, **it's not as easy as they said it would be.** They said the product would sell itself. I believed them because I bought it right away myself…."*

*"I didn't expect the reactions I got from people I knew. **I was shocked and flabbergasted.** "*

*"Man, **if it's this difficult to get five custom-ers, how hard is it going to be to get a thousand,** which is what I need to succeed?"*

Then they ask me:

*"**What am I doing wrong?**"*

People who have substantial business track records are among those who are the most surprised. Over dinner one evening, a former CEO of one of the largest companies in the industry confided:

*"I have high level corporate friends who always had high self-esteem and great confidence in themselves. Then they got into our industry. **Their self-esteem took a big hit because**"*

they weren't used to the personal rejection. Many of them didn't get past it[3].

And they quit in droves.

But that was before.

Enter Three Scripts

Nine months, four agreements and three scripts later, some people's tunes have changed. Their product sales volume is increasing 20 to 30 percent a month. They're getting orders from two to five out of ten people they call, and they're getting larger orders. But probably best of all, they're having fun doing it. And many have gotten their old confidence back.

In their own words:

"Seven out of ten dead customers I called jumped back on auto order. I can't believe how easy it is with this new approach."

-- Jo Ann L, Mannatech

---

[3] Personal communication from former Shaklee president Bob Shults, in June 2003 at a leaders' conference sponsored by Shaklee corporate to which the author was invited as a trainer.

"This week I spoke to 13 people and I got 2 auto-ship customers and 3 referrals, one of whom is a health club owner. **Nothing like this has ever happened to me before. It's fun to work now."**

-- Sandra P, Isagenix

"I talked to 43 people and got 3 new customers and 8 referrals. Plus 6 people said they'd give my number to people they knew were interested. I was shocked. **It makes me feel great."**

-- Jan H, Melaleuca

"I got 3 sales this week talking to 9 old customers. Nothing like that has ever happened to me before this script. **I was stunned.   This is wonderful."**

-- Veronica L, Mannatech

"I'm excited about the new customers I'm getting with my new script because they so much more fit who I am and how I work my business. I want people who care about the rainforest or blind children in Tibet or other good causes and want part of their phone payment to go to such causes. I've always been good at getting and

6

keeping customers, but **now I'm getting the ones I enjoy. Delicious!**

-- *Jacqueline F, Excel*

"In the eight years I've been in marketing, my Mom has never shown interest in any product I've ever sold. Sure, she'd say, 'Oh, that's nice honey,' but she never bought. Then I changed my approach like you taught us in class, and **after my 30-second script, she said "Order me some of that." I was in shock. ...** *"*

--*Spencer L, ForMor*

And Pat gained access to 50 Moms:

"I knew someone who was involved with Mom's Day Out Programs...I called her and used the script I learned yesterday. It was perfect! After a few questions, **she invited me to do a presentation for 50 moms! ..."**

-- *Pat T, Life Force*

The following are participants in a weekly 90-minute Study Hall we set up for Shaklee reps at their request, to help them practice and do what they had learned in the Three Scripts class.[4] To hear these comments in their own voices, click on this link *http://www.whowho911.com/3scripts_studyhall.html.*

"I'm having too much fun. My whole life has changed this week. I went to a Chamber mixer last night and talked to 28 people face to face. Before, I used to be terrified of mixers. I wouldn't have gone for fear that someone would ask me what I do and I'd trip over my answer.

"I also called all 55 people to whom I had sent flyers for a meeting, and talked to 30. I wouldn't have done that before. Plus I made 38 calls to catalog people and spoke to 20.

"Of all the 78 people I talked to, I revived 6 dead people, made 18 "program" sales instead of single bottles, and sold two air units. My sales went up almost $1,000 this week. The dead people hadn't ordered in years and didn't even remember who I was. Their reaction to my script was: 'Isn't that wonderful. That's just what I need...'

---

[4] We now run Study Halls for Three Scripts graduates from all companies. Check the Resource page at the end of this book for Three Scripts classes and Study Hall schedules.

"My whole demeanor, who I am, has changed. What I have to offer is simple. This is amazingly fun."

-- Miriam G

"I did $1,200 in business in one day. ***In my 31 years in business I've never had a day like that, ever.*** *The reason I took the class is because I've been wanting to call these people and didn't know what to say. Now I just call them..."*

-- Mary A

"I made 42 calls, talked to 21 people and made 12 sales, plus one business appointment with a person I had been trying to get to for some time. My new script opened that door. ***I don't know when I've ever had that success... It's wonderful.***"

-- Marceil F

"Seven orders came in from the messages I left. I used the message script we learned how to create in class... One woman dug her catalog out of the trash while I was on the phone, screaming, 'I found it, I found it! I want some of that pain

*stuff...' I got two orders, each almost $500, **and most of the other orders were higher than usual.***"

--Marjorie L

*"I made 50 calls, spoke with 29 people and got 10 orders. But the most exciting thing I did was **I finally opened my mouth at the end of my doctor's appointment, something I never had the nerve to do.** At the end of our conversation about our "natural alternative to Botox" (a phrase Kim created for me in class), my doctor asked me, "What do you want to do – set up a display?"! **Being 73 years old and looking 50 (according to the nurse) is finally paying off...** "*

-- Pat P

These and hundreds more have learned how to reach out to people who were just like them, in very specific ways. For example, one person sought out parents of children who were picky eaters, who worried that their kids were not getting the right nutrition. Another asked for someone who had achy hands and neck from working with their hands all the time, and someone else asked for people who wanted to find a way to get rid of the lines between their eyes without doing surgery or Botox.

They learned to ask for people with similar concerns or symptoms, who were ready to do something about it.

They learned to lead with their own hot button, not look for someone else's. And guess who's responding? **People with the same hot buttons.** It's as though those people heard someone calling them — describing a fix for a situation they too, want to do something about.

If you learned to approach consumers like that and get similar results, do you think you could get 100 customers in 100 days? Would 200 days be OK too?

Surprise! $ for Customers

Let's do something right now that I do at the beginning of all my classes. In the space below, write down how much you spend every month on the products or services that you and your family use.

Every month I spend $_____ on the products/ services for use in my household[5]

Now, multiply that number by 100 customers to see what your monthly sales volume would be.

$_____ x 100 customers = **$_____**

(your monthly order)   **(monthly sales volume from 100 customers)**

Your monthly sales volume is the amount of money you are giving your company each month. They wouldn't have it without your customers.

Now multiply your sales volume by the average percentage your company pays you on customer sales, to see what your monthly income would be.

$_____ x _____ % = **$_____**

(monthly sales volume from 100 customers)   (% company pays you)   **(monthly income from 100 customers)**

---

[5] Do NOT include any amount you buy JUST to qualify for commissions or bonuses.

That would be the start. What if you continued working and got 300 customers in 300 days – in a year or so. How much would you make? Write that number here.

> Above monthly income x 3 = $_____
>
> **(monthly income from <u>300</u> customers)**

To summarize:

> 100 customers ordering what I order monthly would pay
>
>   me $_____
>
> 300 customers ordering what I order monthly would pay
>
>   me $_____

That's with or without your downline. Notice that? ☺

Mary Jane's Story

Here's what happened to someone who took up the challenge of getting 100 customers in 100 days after taking the class.

"At the time I was introduced to the Three Scripts class, I was someone who had no experience whatsoever in marketing.... I was an executive assistant in corporate America, and had been

content for years with my weekly paycheck, company health insurance, my 9-to-5 workday, and luncheons with office friends. I accepted driving in traffic and corporate politics as part of my way of life.

"It happened that at the time I was extremely overweight. I had tried everything and finally found a product that helped me lose 153 pounds in 6 months! I was so excited about it I decided to sell it.

"I did 'sales' just like they said to do, online and off line. Five people out of every 200 bought something once. The rest just took up a lot of time.

"Then, my friend Ruth Johnson introduced me to Kim's Three Scripts class which she does over the phone.

"During my first day of class, I created my "first date" script. While Kim went on to the next person, I received an email from a lady who wanted to find out about my program, but wasn't sure it is was right for her.

"So I cut and pasted my new one-paragraph script that I had just created in class and BINGO!!! I get this letter back within 5 minutes. The lady said, "This is the program for me and my husband. It sounds just like us…" And to my surprise she ordered

14

$400 worth of products! The commission I made on that order paid for Kim's class.

"Since the Three Scripts class in July 2003...I feel extremely confident selling my product. I used to talk a lot and give

too much information. Now it's short and sweet and it works! Now I have time to play with my dog and be a wife, and hang out with friends. I HAVE MY LIFE BACK, and my family has me back...

"Kim challenged us to get a 100 customers in a 100 days, and guess what? I did more than that! I got over 100 customers in 60 days, and they're on a monthly program, just like cable TV! My check went from $986 to over $5000 within five months. I'll be forever grateful to my friend Ruth Johnson for introducing me to Kim."

--Mary Jane M, Take Shape for Life, 9-10-03

Taking this approach requires radically changing much of what you've learned to say to people about your product or service. But that doesn't surprise you, does it?

According to Einstein:

"The significant problems we face cannot be solved at the same level of thinking we were at when we created them."[6]

---

[6] http://www.jokemonster.com/quotes/quotes/a/q130982.html

Prelude to a New Level of Peformance: Four Agreements for Marketers

> *"If you can begin to live your life with these agreements, the transformation in your life will be amazing. You will see the drama of hell disappear right before your very eyes. Instead ... you will be creating a new dream – your personal dream of heaven."*

> Don Miguel Ruiz.
> *The Four Agreements 1997*, p. 23

on Miguel has changed the lives of the millions of people who have read his little book and have made the four life agreements with themselves. There are now little groups all over the country who meet and discuss the four agreements and support each other in creating new meaningful lives.

I won't discuss Don Miguel's agreements here. His book is a fast and easy read.

The four agreements I offer you instead are for marketers. They were, unbeknownst to me until now, the foundation of my sales performance, and apparently that of successful marketers throughout the world. They are agreements I subconsciously made with myself regarding how I interacted with the marketplace – the people who were in the running to buy my thing. These four agreements gave rise to the words I used.

The first agreement preserved my self-esteem; the second made sure I didn't lose the few good prospects by mistake; the third popped open the minds of the ones who would buy; and the fourth guaranteed me wild success.

Ready?

First Agreement:

Let go the 9 in 10 who won't buy.

The Odds of Making a Sale

About one in ten average people appear to be real candidates for a good product or service. That means nine out of ten just won't buy, no matter what you say or do, no matter who you are. You've discovered this, yes? ☹

In direct marketing, we take the risk of hearing and feeling all those *No*'s. It's enough to make one really depressed. Or phone phobic. Or reach for an adult beverage.

What percent of the people whom you've contacted have bought, not counting parents or friends who just wanted to do you a favor in the beginning?

Most people I've talked to say it's one in ten or twenty. ☹ Does that square with your experience?

The numbers are way worse for the huge companies who spend millions of dollars on TV or radio. But unlike us, they don't hurt like we do, because they don't hear or feel the sting of all the *No*'s they get. They have no personal contact with their prospective customers.

Mass marketers go for the biggest audiences possible, so that the tiny fraction of a percent that responds will make marketing their product worthwhile. The last Super Bowl had over one hundred million viewers. [7] *The Sopranos* have 20 million and counting.[8]

Companies pay for the chance to reach such a big audience. A 60-second time slot on the 2004 Super Bowl cost advertisers around $2.3 million.[9] Ads typically cost an additional $500,000 to $1 million to produce. And what percent of that giant audience actually goes out and

---

[7] *New York Times*, 2.3.04, p C5.

[8] Godin, S. (2003), *o* p. 42.

[9] *New York Times* , 2.3.04, p. C5.

buys that breakfast cereal or computer they see advertised? Would you believe it's often a mere fraction of a percent – less than one in 100, more often one in 1000, or even worse.   But if someone can pay for enough exposure, those tiny percentages can turn into big dollars.

Few individuals can scrape up the funds required to reach the millions of people it takes to get enough of them to place an order or go to a store to buy. That's why direct marketing is so popular.

Question: When you decided to do network marketing, did **you** know about the odds of making a sale?

More likely, like most people, you're focused on how great your product or service is, and how much Mom or Sarah or Tom needs it, and how great it's going to be when they start using it, right? You might even think of all those obese people out there whom you don't even know, and what a favor you're going to be doing all of them by showing them your great new weight loss product. Wahoo!

Then most of them say "No thanks." ☹

The People Who Don't Buy

What's wrong with those people anyway??? Doesn't **everyone** want to lose weight and have more energy? Or have free long distance with local service? Or change their lives like you changed yours? What's wrong with those 9 in 10 you've discovered don't want your thing, when you can see they need it?

Here's the sad truth about marketing. According to Seth Godin, marketing guru and author of the recent bestseller *Purple Cow*: "Most people can't buy your product. Either they don't have the money, they don't have the time, or they don't want it."[10]

While that may be true, it seems almost impossible to accept that people who need it and can afford it, don't want it. They're falling asleep at their desk at four in the afternoon but won't try something to keep them alert. Or they complain they can't fit in an

---

[10] Godin, S (2003), p. 10

airplane seat but aren't interested in hearing about a new weight program. Or they complain about their over-priced long distance phone bill and then say they won't switch from their trusty local phone company.

It must be me, most people figure. Maybe I've left out some important information. Either I've said too much or said the wrong thing, or maybe I haven't spent enough time with them.

What am I doing wrong ???

Well, maybe nothing! I discovered that for the 9 in 10 "won't-buys", it really wasn't anything I did or didn't do. For nearly all, the reason seemed to be that their values and priorities were different, and I was just discovering that – one person at a time.

Won't Buy Type 1: Not on Their Radar.

Did you used to think that the things you value are what other people value too? Like looking good, getting rid of aches and pains, or playing A-level tennis until you're 96. That's why it seems so reasonable to expect that people who are overweight, or look old before their time, or are tired often, should be happy to buy something that will make them look or feel better.

I wish. People have their own Change List with their own priorities on it—things that are "on their radar". When their radar spots those things, they'll buy. However, things that are not on their Change List will not be on their radar and they won't buy.

And who can say a list is right or wrong? It's fabulous if your thing is on their radar, but if it isn't, bye-bye baby. No time for dragging or therapy right now. Otherwise, how will you ever make it in your lifetime?

John T, for example, is 48, in generally good health, and still fairly strong from his football days. We catch up with him at a cafe, where he's sipping a latte and munching an almond croissant with his friendly wife Julie. The subject of health and weight comes up. John, gently patting his growing pot belly, volunteers: "One thing about getting up there is I can do more of this (waving arm around café). I'm married, not planning on any affairs, and I can eat and drink what I like now. I don't overdo it, but I'm willing to live with this (patting his belly) so that I can do these things..." Smiles mischievously at his slim wife, dunking his croissant into his latte...

How good of a prospect is John for you if you're promoting a weight loss program or product? *He represents the first few of those 9 in 10 who won't buy your weight program.*

Now you must decide: Do you want to do therapy on John or find customers who feel like you do about the weight issue to begin with?

Won't-Buy Type 2: Still on Their Vent List

People have two running lists in their minds: the Change List and the Vent List.

Items on the Vent List are those about which someone often complains, whines or makes jokes, and even beats themselves up for, but otherwise does little or nothing about. Items on the Change List are those about which someone is actively doing something.

Test it. What did you have on your Change List in the last year that you succeeded in changing? List those things here, then give yourself a hug for changing!

```
┌─────────────────────────────────────────────┐
│                                               │
│        YOUR CHANGE LIST SUCCESSES             │
│              _____                      │
│                                               │
│             (for the last year)               │
│                                               │
│   ☺  _____  │
│                                               │
│   ☺  _____  │
│                                               │
│   ☺  _____  │
│                                               │
│                                               │
└─────────────────────────────────────────────┘
```

What do you have on your Vent List? List those things below, and remember, don't beat yourself up for not changing them. They haven't been on your Change List.

MY VENT LIST

☹ _____

☹ _____

☹ _____

☹ _____

☹ _____

☹ _____

☹ _____

Go ahead and select one thing to switch from your Vent to your Change List right now. Put a big star by it and see what happens.

Venting Story

At a spa in Mexico a few months ago, one of the guests was saying how she loved the warm weather, and how much she hated the cold and windy winters in Chicago. She had lived there the past 20 years. "I can't believe I still live there," she said. "I hate the wind and cold and every winter I tell myself I have to move somewhere warm, but I find myself there again the next winter. What is wrong with me? I keep on saying it every year and suffer every year because that's where I find myself again!"

I was happy to pipe in that her move from Chicago might just be on her Vent List, that's all. Doesn't everyone need to vent about things? That was one of hers. When she was really ready to do something, I told her, she'd move it to her Change List and that's when she'd do something about it. In the meantime, vent away. Venting is good for the soul. And don't beat on yourself about it, because now you know what list it's on. The thing's a venter, not a changer.

She beamed. Said she felt much better now, could vent in peace, and would decide this week at the spa, if she'd move it to the Change List or not.

She left a few days later, and as she was leaving, she waved at me and said: "I've decided to move 'leaving Chicago' to my Change List. I've called ahead and put my place on the market. I'm taking a job here. Thanks!"

Of course things don't always turn out that way. How many of you have been fooled by people who complain about certain things, then, when offered a chance to fix it with your program or product, they don't bite?   Which list do you think that was on for them? And who do you think decides which list it's on? You? Or they? Arghhhh.

Recent studies report that 64% of Americans are overweight or obese. Ask yourself, how many of those people do you think are actively doing something about their weight problem?   Instead of just venting about it? For how many is it mostly on their Vent List? That's another few of those 9 in 10 who won't bite.

Can you accept those stats? That 9 in 10 who didn't bite before probably won't do so now, no matter how great your product or service is?

If so, take a minute now and make the First Agreement with yourself.

First Agreement

Let go the
9 in 10 who
won't buy

Close your eyes and say it
out loud, with all your heart.

Second Agreeement:
No more seller talk.

S o, what about the one in ten who is ready for what you have? How do you know which one it is? And how do you make sure you don't lose that one by accident?

Many people have confided that they're certain that they lost a sale or two because they talked too much or because they said the wrong thing. Has that happened to you? Ugh. Here's advice from the biggest and brightest in advertising.

On May 21, 2003, *USA Today* asked the new chairman of one of the world's largest ad agencies, Young & Rubicam (Y&R), this question:

> *"The biggest challenge in this [advertising] business is creating messages that win over*

*consumers for clients. What's your answer to
that?"*

Y&R Chairman Ann Fudge, whose clients
include Ford Motor, Sears, AT&T and other giant
companies, said:

*"You always have to put yourself in the
shoes of the consumer. It's not what we
think, it's what the consumer thinks."*

Do you agree with that? That what the consumer
thinks is more important than what the seller (or
advertiser) thinks - about a particular product or service?

OK. So here is the big question: How do you
put yourself in the shoes of the consumer when you are
the seller? It's tricky. Consider this:

Can you tell when a seller starts talking?

Do you tend to go towards that person, or away
from them?

Join the rest of the world. When sellers start
talking, almost no one listens anymore. Apparently,
everyone can tell when a seller starts talking or writing,
because they all talk the same way.

Sales people and advertisers have developed a special language all their own – I call it "seller talk". Like baby talk, it's immediately recognizable.

Seems like everyone wants to escape from seller talk as quickly as possible. Don't you?

Just like millions of people watching TV use TiVo[11] to zap the ads. TiVo has become a cult gizmo for people who can't stand the seller talk ads are filled with. The minute an ad starts, they zap it with TiVo, which can also record the programs minus the ads!

In the person-to-person direct sales world, people can't use TiVo to zap the person talking seller talk. Instead, they change channels in their minds. They tune out and start thinking of ways to get away from the seller. Have you done that?

Say you meet someone at a gathering of some kind, and you ask them "So, Lulu, what do you do?"

She bubbles: "I'm a wellness consultant. We market unique, patented, scientifically proven

---

[11] Erica Taub, "How Do I Love Thee, TiVo?", 2004.

nutraceuticals."

What do you want to do now? …

Well others do the same thing when YOU launch into seller talk. They do a mental TiVo. You can tell when they do it, can't you? You're doing your spiel, and suddenly, the other person's eyes glaze over. That's the sign they've TiVo-ed you. They're now frantically thinking of a way to get away from you politely (sometimes). They'll say, "Oh that's nice. Say what's for lunch?" Or "I have to go to the restroom now…talk to you later." Or, if you're on the phone and they don't know you, they just hang up. And that's the end of that.

Most people run from seller talk. It's as though the words have suddenly given you B O or a severe case of bad breath. That may be why many of the students in my Three Scripts classes have confessed that they dread being asked "What do you do?" and avoid going to mixers. No one wants to be known as someone who has B O…

How can you market your products and services without contracting seller's B O ?

Here are three tell-tale signs of seller talk. See if you recognize them.

Scent of a Seller

Three signs of seller talk:

1.   Generalities

Generalities are words and phrases that speak to no one in particular. **If the words you use do not speak to anyone in particular, who will respond? ...**

For example, "I have health and wellness products." Or "I do telecommunications."

Did you hear anything that caused you to perk up your ears? Did you lean closer to the seller to hear more? Or did those words trigger an "Oh that's nice" or "Who cares" attitude? And you moved right on to something else more relevant, like "What's for lunch?"

Dull, nondescript, abstract words like 'health' or 'nutrition' create nothing in anyone's mind – no image, no feelings; just blah. Vague phrases like 'natural health program' or 'weight loss program' or 'communications system' are also totally boring, aren't they? Does seeing them or hearing them right now make you sit right up and think: 'I want to know more about that!'?

Generalities make no impact because they speak to no one in particular; they leave no impression. They get no one's attention, and, therefore, no one buys.

2.   Techno-babble

Techno-babble is jargon, shop-talk.   Like "patented, scientifically proven nutraceuticals". They're words a 13-year old would not understand. Sellers like to use technical product names, or the name of their company – words a normal consumer just glazes over.

As a consumer, you wouldn't use them either. How many of you would go to a store and say, "I want a proven, unique, patented nutraceutical, please"? How many consumers OUTSIDE of your company have ever heard of your company?... Ergo, both your company name and what your product is scientifically, are techno-babble to most consumers.

Remember what Ms. Fudge said, "It's not what we think, it's what the consumer thinks."

Names of diseases are techno-babble; symptoms of diseases are not. For example, most people don't know what fibromyalgia is or feels like. They might identify, though, with achy muscles and being too tired to get out of bed. Describing symptoms might open a consumer's mind to what else you might say; naming a disease would not in most cases.

Naming diseases also puts you at risk of making medical claims. Some people have awesome stories of recovery from serious conditions such as cancer or schizophrenia, and want to give others the opportunity to rise from the dead too. It's best, however, to temper that enthusiasm when you first approach someone. For several reasons:

First, you are a Seller, and your credibility is, by definition, questionable, no matter how true your story is.

Second, people are different and you never know whether someone's body will respond like yours did, or if someone will take the product the same way that you did, or has different life circumstances that will affect their recovery.

And third, only MD's are licensed to treat such conditions, so you may be accused of practicing medicine without a license. A remote possibility, but one that companies are very careful to avoid.

3. Hype

Unbelievable claims, that sound inflated, excessive or extravagant. Misleading ploys. What self-respecting consumer would respond to it?

I know that no one reading this has any intention of using hype. But **what if you don't know you're doing it?** As the seller, you have to watch what you say. You cannot say things you could say if you were not benefiting financially from the product you're talking about.

Say you feel like you got your life back after taking your product. You can say anything you want to anyone, and it won't be perceived as hype because you're not making any money on it. This is like recommending a restaurant you don't own. However, once you decide to go into business and sell the product that helped you so much, the same things you said before now come across as hype. The fact that you could make money from a sale automatically gives you a hidden agenda and people will be more cautious about what you say. They often walk away.

Three things in seller talk usually feel like hype to a consumer: promises, chestbeating and 'screaming'.

4.   Promises

Claims or predictions are the promises sellers make about the benefits of their products or services. For example: This will prevent cancer. Or this will save you 50%. Or this will get rid of your aches and pains in a few weeks. Or you'll be able to go off your medications. Or you'll be getting the best nutrition available. They're promises that a seller makes to a consumer about whom they know nothing, or claims about an outcome they do not control.

Recently I got a call from a telemarketer who opened the conversation with: "Hello Ms. Klaver, I can save you 50% on your phone bill. Are you interested?"

My first thought was: He's a complete amateur. How does he know I'm not someone with a $10 a month phone bill? Or even if he got my name from a list of people who make lots of long distance calls, he didn't know what I was paying, so how would he know if he could save me anything, much less 50%? It might even be more.

Who can tell what's on someone's Change List, what someone's circumstances are, or whether someone's body will respond? Who can tell the future? All empty promises. Hype.

5.   Chestbeating

Even if a seller truly believes that their product is the best in the history of the world, saying it sounds like chestbeating to a consumer. If a product changed my life, I would certainly think it is the most powerful on earth, but, the question is, will the consumer believe me or think I'm chestbeating? ...

Whenever a seller uses words like: "This is the *most exciting, fantastic, amazing, wonderful, cheapest, highest quality thing out there"* about what they're selling, consumers feel hyped.

Same with talking about the company. "This company cares about you." "The doctors on our advisory panel say it's the best product in the history of the world."

Doesn't everyone say that about their thing? If EVERYONE says it, what's to distinguish you?

Worse, few consumers believe it. Why? Because they're aware that these doctors are paid by the company or that they invented the product. So, what else would they say? They're like paid informants or researchers who are financed by the manufacturers of products they're researching. Their opinions are paid for, and therefore, suspect. This is not about truth but about believability.

6.   Screaming

Screaming is overstating. Sellers overstate when they use superlatives or exaggerations, such as:

- "It's the best, or the most …

- "You'll be totally blown away…"

- Quick fixes

In print or online, in addition to words that exaggerate, it's the "tabloid look":

- Too red

- Too bold

- Exclamation points

- Inappropriate use of capital letters

Strunk and White, who have been the bible of writing style forever, say:

> "When you overstate, readers will be
> instantly on guard, and everything that has
> preceded your overstatement as well as
> everything that follows will be suspect in
> their minds because they have lost
> confidence in your judgment or your
> poise." [12]

The same words of caution were in *The New York Times*'s "Business Digest" column on December 22, 2003, beginning the piece "Cautionary Tale on Marketing":

---

[12] Strunk and White, p. 73.

"Partners for Hologenix, a company that makes clothes with a proprietary fiber that promises to relieve aches and pains, have a marketing challenge. The fiber, called Holofiber, is expensive and sales of clothing made with it have not been brisk. And therein lies a cautionary tale for anyone trying to market a "scientific breakthrough" item **in an age when claims of "all new" or "revolutionary" fall on increasingly jaded ears…"** (p. C1)

Promises, chestbeating and screaming have three strikes against them.

One, can you, by yourself, fulfill the promise or live up to the expectations you've built up about what they will experience?

Two, doesn't every seller make the same promises and say the same things about their product?

And three, EVEN IF the thing you say happens to be true, you lose instant credibility the moment they find out you're selling it.

Think of how you react to someone you're having lunch with, who's gushing about something to you, and afterwards you discover they're selling it… How do you feel about their gushing now?

My students have replied:

"Used."

"Manipulated."

"Lied to."

"They didn't really care about me. They just wanted to sell me their product."

If you don't mention up front that you are marketing the product, when they finally find out, everything you said about its wonders will come into question. Even if everything you said were true, the truth is suddenly suspect.

Examples of Seller talk

Here are five of the hundreds of unedited approach scripts people sent in – what they <u>were</u> saying to win over consumers.

In each class, we had a contest to decide who had the worst seller script. (The winner got a free book or tape set.) One would say they had the worst one, then someone else would insist they had the worst one, then yet another student would offer an even worse one. We laughed a lot.

Have someone else read the scripts below to you OUT LOUD and notice how you react. As you hear each one, ask: "Does this make me sit right up and want more info?" **Hearing it will kick in your consumer ears.**

Scene:

Potential consumers and sellers meet up. After the usual niceties:

CONSUMER 1
So what do you do?

> **SELLER 1**
> I have my own home-based business, and what I do is educate people on how they can protect and build their immune systems with glyconutritionals. These are the same nutrients as in mother's breast milk, and we're supposed to be able to continue getting them in our

46

food, but don't. So now we have autoimmune diseases on the rise such as cancer, etc.

~ ~

CONSUMER 2
What do you do?

SELLER 2
I'm in the wellness industry. We distribute products that help people get well and stay that way.

CONSUMER 2
What do you sell?

SELLER 2
I represent a research and development company on the cutting edge of scientific technology which has discovered how cells communicate with each other. The products we distribute actually allow the body to function as God intended; that is to fight disease, get well and stay well.

~ ~

CONSUMER 3
What do you do?

SELLER 3:

I help people find solutions to their problems through safe, natural, effective products of God's good creation.

CONSUMER 3

What do you sell?

SELLER 3

I sell a full line of safe, natural, and effective health care, home care, personal care, and pure air and water products.

CONSUMER 4

What do you do?

SELLER 4

I am a Wellness Coach. I educate people on how to make wise choices in the wellness marketplace.

CONSUMER 4

What do you sell?

SELLER 4

I have chosen Company X products as they embody the highest standards in the wellness industry for purity, potency & efficacy.

~ ~ ~ ~ ~ ~ ~ ~ ~ ~ ~ ~ ~ ~ ~ ~ ~ ~ ~

CONSUMER 5
What do you do?

> **SELLER 5**
> I market products that are unconsciously purchased and habitually consumed. Mary, what is so exciting about our business is that our customers are already using our products. All we have to do is ask them to try our brand for 90 days, especially, if they like the idea of helping a variety of philanthropic causes, rather than an over-the-hill quarterback or some has-been starlet. Oh yes, our products range all the way from Local Service to DSL, our newest product...

Did you feel the urge to buy after hearing any of these? Did your eyes glaze over? Did your attention wander?

The authors of these scripts didn't mind being voted the worst script in their classes, because they knew they'd get a brand new one. And besides, they won a prize!

Exercise: Review the three things that make up the scent of a seller in the box below. Then, line

through all the seller talk you notice in the scripts above.
What's left? … ☹

The Scent of a Seller

1. **Generalities**
   (general, vague, nondescript, abstract
   words that speak to no one in
   particular)

2. **Techno-babble**
   (names of products, companies,
   diseases, technical terms)

3. **Hype**
   • Promises
   • Chestbeating
   • Screaming

Now, are you ready to make the Second Agreement with
yourself?

Second Agreement

No more seller talk

Close your eyes and say it out loud, with all your heart.

Third Agreeement:
Lead with **YOUR** hot button

How do we reach that special one in ten who would buy our thing if they knew what it could do for them?

First, we make sure we don't turn them off and make them change channels. Live by the Second Agreement. '*No more seller talk*' is our new mantra and we monitor ourselves like hawks to swallow any seller words that might reappear just out of old habit.

Don't worry if you hear yourself still sounding a bit like a seller bear once in a while. It happens. The old habit will slowly disappear the more you practice the Second Agreement. It may take a while, but soon, it will become second nature and you'll know that the people who don't respond to you are probably one of the 9 in 10, no matter what you said. At least not now.

When we eliminate all seller talk from our product introductions, we're often left with nothing to say! Test this on your own product introduction script. Cross out all words and phrases that are generalities, techno-babble, or hype. What do you have left??? ...

That's right ... ☹

So, what do we say instead? -- The same thing we normally say when we want someone's attention. We call their name.

Picture a group of people downtown where you live, and you announce: "Everyone named 'Harry', please step forward". If you spoke Harry's name loudly and clearly enough, wouldn't all the Harry's step forward wondering what you had in store for them?

Would you expect the people named James to respond too? Maybe a few Jameses would step up wondering what the Harry's were getting, and thinking they might get in on the action too. If you asked for "everyone who wears a size eight shoe" or "anyone who recycles" don't you think the size eighters and the recyclers might perk up, curious why they were singled out? Perhaps they might even feel special.

People go by lots of different names – Christian, redhead, prefer alternatives to drugs, have achy joints, etc.

OK, you say. That makes sense, but how can we call their name if we don't know it??? ... You're right. It's tricky. But there's a way ☺

Forget Their Hot Buttons

You've probably heard that your job as a direct marketer is to find a prospect's hot button, so you can push it and make the sale. You may do it already, not just when you're marketing but in the course of daily life. For example, when you want someone to do something they might resist. When you want to get your teenage daughter to pick up her room, or your husband to babysit while you're working, don't you bribe them with something you know they'll like?

Some companies give their sales people the "FORM" approach to help them find someone's hot button. It works like this: Strike up a conversation about **F**amily, **O**ccupation, **R**ecreation or **M**oney (or Mission). One of those areas of interest will contain their hot button, which they will talk about in some detail, allowing you to weave that interest into your pitch about your product or service. When you find their hot button, you push it to make a sale.

One lady in class confessed: "I'm not enjoying meeting people anymore. I feel like a piranha.[13] I'm afraid they're seeing me as a barracuda coming for them."

Why? Because deep down she knew she was acting like a barracuda. She was well aware of the real reason she was pursuing people, and she knew it was not pure. And of course, eventually the barracuda has to show its teeth – she would have to reveal that she had something to sell them. The whole class was sympathetic and many felt the same.

---

[13] A tropical American freshwater fish that is voraciously carnivorous and often attacks and destroys living animals. From *The American Heritage® Dictionary of the English Language.*

Consider this scenario. Say you're an animal lover, maybe even an activist for animal rights. Imagine that you meet someone and make friends with them. Talking on the phone, meeting at a café, etc. Over lunch, the person tells you about an upcoming hunting trip he's all gung-ho on. How will you, an animal person who loves living creatures, react to someone who kills animals for sport? And you've just spent three weeks trying to make friends with this person, for your business! Arghhh. ☹

Well, good news. From now on, you can forget all about finding other people's hot buttons. How about we find YOUR hot button instead? That thing that YOU are concerned about or something that happened in YOUR life – which is the reason you do your program.

Your Hot Button

"How can MY hot button turn someone else on?" you might ask. The same way that asking for people with the same name as yours gets them to perk up their ears and say "Oh, that's me too!"

Someone named Mary who calls for other people named Mary will get the Mary's. Olivia will get the Olivia's, and Harry will get the Harry's. Don't you have a kind of instant relationship when someone you meet has the same name you do? You have many other names that are just as much of a hot button for you as your first name. We'll show you words and phrases that describe your hot button in enough detail so that people can identify with it, and respond just as quickly as when they hear their proper name.

Consider interest groups like Mothers Against Drunk Driving, VW Bug Owners, Overeaters Anonymous, Tibetan Buddhists, or Environmental Defenders. Interest groups exist because certain people have similar hot buttons, which drive them to join, support and grow those groups.[14]

---

[14] Google interest groups number more than 70,000.

So it is with you and your customers. YOUR hot button, as it relates to your product experience, will draw them as though you had called their name.

Once you find your own hot button – the reason you fell in love with your product or service—you'll be able to ask for people just like you, who buy for the same reasons you did.

You'll be calling them by name and it will be YOUR hot button name. This is leading with your hot button. And because it is your name, you'll be speaking from your truth – YOUR CONSUMER TRUTH. Fortunately, there are hundreds of thousands of people with the same hot button as yours – more than enough to keep any direct marketer busy filling orders for years.

You'll be putting yourself in your consumer shoes again, like Ann Fudge, the chairman of the largest U.S ad agency, said to do. You'll be replacing Seller talk with Consumer talk. And you'll be able to do this on the phone, in person, as a basis for any ad copy, TV and radio spots, flyers, direct mail, business cards, brochure labels, answering machine messages and email signatures. For both warm and cold markets.

How to Lead with YOUR Hot Button

The trick is learning to state your hot button name so clearly that your prospects hear it distinctly. How do we call out something that is as clear as "Olivia, are you there?" or "All Kim's on deck!" or "Do you know anyone named Harry"?

The formula for doing that is laid out in the next section. Here are the five strategies that guide that formula.

1. **First, find your truth.** It takes going inside and back in time, for that part of you and your experience that's related to the thing you're now selling. It takes recalling sometimes painful or embarrassing circumstances in juicy detail. It takes being willing to tell about it clearly enough so that the listener feels the pain, the need, or the excitement you felt then. If they do, or if they know of someone who does, they usually step

59

forward and say, "That sounds like me. What do you have?"

2. **Be honest always.** Tell them right off that you market your thing, or are introducing it to people in the area. You're not sharing it, or making friendly suggestions. Of course you're friendly, but if you're taking their money, you are, like it or not, selling it!

If you say it simply and honestly, they will accept it, because they do want to buy things. They just want to buy from someone with integrity, whom they trust enough to take advice from, and who they perceive is offering something they want.

This is not like recommending a restaurant or a movie, unless you happen to own that restaurant or movie theater.

Remember, even if you love your product, you have a financial interest in the outcome of your recommendation and, therefore, when it comes out, your ravings will be suspect.

You don't have that problem for your favorite restaurant or movie.

3. **Don't project your results onto others.** Just because you had success with your thing doesn't mean the whole world will. People are different and they react to the same things in different ways. So, you relate your experience as an instance of how your thing worked for you and put the ball in their court as to whether it might work for them or not. That way, they feel they are in control of the decision to buy and that you are more like their trusted advisor instead of a hypey seller. If they identify with your experience and values, and if they want to see the same changes in their bodies or lives, they will step up and say, "That sounds like me. Tell me more."

4. **Pretend it's your first date**. Opening a potential customer's mind to your thing is like going on a first date. Remember your first date? You open the kimono just a little, then pause and wait for the response. You don't strip down right off, do

you? ... So, tell them just enough to whet their appetite. Let THEM ask for a next date.

5. **Believe in the power of specific words**. HOW you say something may be as important as what you want to convey. The specific words you say can turn people on or off, regardless of how powerful your experience was or how effective your thing is.

   In my classes we worked on each script until the scriptee said, "I love it madly!" and we could tell they meant it. Many said, "I love it madly. It's me…"

   Shall we start on yours?

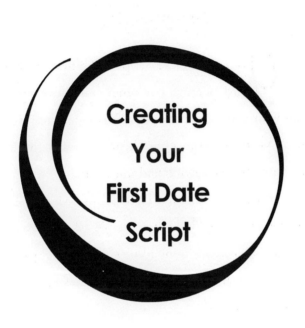

Creating
Your
First Date
Script

Remembering

*Y*our First Date Script is the first thing your prospective customer will hear you say about your product or service. First dates are just first dates. No telling your entire history on that first date. That comes in the second and third date.

You'll use your First Date Script or parts of it in many ways: to respond when people ask you what you do, to introduce your thing to new people, and to create ads, flyers, business cards, voice mail messages, emails and email signatures.

This is not about memorizing something that everyone parrots. It's about learning to use a FORMULA to create your own unique script. If you put an authentic part of yourself in your script, you'll touch certain people and magically open their minds to your product or service.

The formula has two parts: Remembering and Scripting. We do Remembering first. It has five steps:

1)   Remembering how you were **Before** you came across your product or service

2)   Remembering what happened **After** you started using your product or service

3)   Choosing your **Favorite Fix**

4)   Remembering a few **Personal Zingers**

5)   Remembering **the Things You Tried** before you came across your product or service

STEP 1. Before…

Get a pen or pencil and pad of paper, and go to a quiet, comfortable place where you won't be interrupted for about an hour.

When you're there, take a deep relaxing breath and feel like you're daydreaming. Now bring into your mind the products or services that you sell, the ones that you and your family use regularly... what they've done for you and your family that make you happy... Now step back in time… into the **Remembering Room** of your mind.

Remember when you first tried your product or service—*before you started selling it.*

What made you decide to try it? What were the specific things you were suffering from, or were disgusted with, or really needed or wanted to do?

Were you dragging? Feeling old? Have skin or nails that didn't look their best? Did you have achy joints or other health condition that doctors had given up on? Were you spending too much on your phone bill or on lawyers? Were you concerned about chemicals? About the poor quality of food, soil, air or water? Were you concerned about someone in your family? Did you want to play A-tennis until you're 96? Or just have the confidence that you were doing the right thing to stay healthy?

After some gentle nudging for details, here are some of the "before" things that students in my classes came up with:

> I used to fall asleep babysitting my grandchildren
> I used to get really nervous. My heart would start going really fast, like it was going to jump out of my chest and I would feel sweaty like I was going to faint.
> I was often cranky with my family.
> I was always interested in health but had to take Motrin for headaches that wouldn't go away.
> I used to take 7 or 8 supplements a day and didn't know whether they worked or not.
> I was someone who has always had an interest in my health, in eating right and in hitting my peak performance.
> I was someone who could always do a lot of things at the same time and then couldn't do them anymore.

> I was someone who was always active in sports, and then started slowing down, getting sore, needing more rest in between workouts.

> I looked in the mirror and saw wrinkles, a sagging jaw, a double chin, and a big potbelly; I looked like my mother.

> I couldn't run up and down the stairs like I used to.

> I couldn't breathe; I had to bring Kleenex everywhere I went and couldn't go anywhere without my inhaler

> I have so much energy and I do so many things but when I looked in the mirror I didn't recognize that person. She looked so old…

> I had lost my zest for life. I didn't want to do social things anymore like I used to.

> I didn't have a plan to get rid of my credit card debt.

> I worried about how big my phone bill was going to be.

> I didn't want to pay $200 an hour for an attorney.

Many students at first felt a resistance to recounting those circumstances, saying something vague like they were "tired" or had "no energy". But that tells no one anything they can relate to specifically. After all, "tired" for you might mean you need to lie down during the day, whereas for someone else it means they can't run their usual 15 miles a day. 'Tired' is boring.

Some felt that the situations were too personal, or too painful, or sometimes, not impressive enough. Or that it was nobody's business to know the real reason.

With some encouragement, however, one student would find the courage to share a deep dark secret and then everyone would see how we transformed those "personal zingers" into a first date script. Then it would start happening for everyone in the class and people couldn't wait for their turn.

If you feel the same resistance, remember that no one is privy to your thoughts or to what you will be writing down. This part is only for you. So you can drop your guard about it and remember when…

If Your Reason Was Financial

A few people have said that they started taking their product not because they had any situation related to the product but because they were in a financial bind and wanted to do the business to earn money. There will be a time to relate that story; now is not the time. (I'll tell you how in a later section.)

This is the time to recall your Before and After for your product or service regardless of why you started using it.

So, instead of remembering your financial situation before you started taking the product, remember what the product did for you **after** you started using it for a while. Complete this sentence:

"After I started using the product, I noticed ... "

The improvement in your health or state of mind that you noticed becomes your memory trigger for how you were before taking your product. Then you can complete the sentence:

"Before taking the product I was someone who…"

and you'll be right in the groove.

Triggers and Timeframes

Sometimes it helps to recall what happened in your life that triggered the conditions or problems you were having, and how long ago you started noticing them.

For example, one of the people remembered that she "used to run an infant toddler day care center for years." That's what made her "so tired at night she couldn't do her gardening anymore or her needlework, and her husband got really lonesome."

Or another said "Seven years ago my relationship fell apart, and after the break up, a lot of things went downhill." That's what triggered losing her zest for life and the other things she described. Here are other examples of Befores that include triggers and timeframes:

➢ I ran a medical practice for 25 years, and four years ago when the government got involved, I lost my freedom to run it. I worked longer hours, did more procedures, saw my family less, and made less money. I became a grump at home…

➢ About 3 and a half years ago I pulled some muscles in my arms and chest and then I couldn't work out like I used to. I couldn't even carry groceries or lift my briefcase…

➢ I was healthy and active all my life until I had children…

➢ For 12 years, once a month I used to get cranky and yell at people…

➢ I was healthy most of my life, then about 4 years ago I noticed my joints started getting achy and I'd get these shooting pains up and down my back…

➢ I've had trouble breathing for as long as I can remember…

> After I turned 13, I'd get three to four horrible colds every year...

All of these tell a story because they use PICTURE WORDS. Compare your reaction to these stories to the reaction you'd have if any of these people had just said, "I didn't feel good." If vague words come to you first, like "I was tired," or "I was stressed out," say to yourself:

"What I mean by that is…"

and your mind will come up with a picture of what you're like when you feel tired. Picture words will then emerge for you. If it's too long ago to remember specifics, pick another "Before."

Use the box coming up in a bit to write down your "Before" memories. Start the memories rolling by beginning with: "Before I started using my product (or service) I was someone who…"

Step 2. After

What happened AFTER you began using the product or service? Did your product or service fix or improve one or more of your Before situations?

For example, after some prodding, Nora B of Mannatech remembered that before she came across her product, she was so tired that she used to fall asleep babysitting her grandchildren. After three weeks of using her product she didn't fall asleep babysitting her grandkids anymore. No more embarrassed grandma.

Chuck S of Usana, a pilot, reported that before he started using his product, it would take him two to three days to recover from a trip. He'd be so tired he couldn't do his usual workouts and his wife thought he was boring. After a month of using his product, he could do normal workouts right after a flight and his wife didn't think he was boring anymore.

Sometimes, using your thing may have solved problems you didn't even know you had. For example

Lorna G of Shaklee took a product hoping to resolve her hot flashes. After a month she noticed that her knees didn't ache anymore.

Cheryl B of Ideal Health, who has always been health-conscious, remembered that before she came across her product, "I had a cupboard full of pills and was so confused about what to take I didn't take anything regularly." Then, she remembered that AFTER taking a test, which gave her six things that fit her body, she threw out her old pills and didn't feel confused anymore.

The fixes don't have to be dramatic; they just have to be true.

Just one thing can make a difference in someone's life. For example, not needing an inhaler anymore made a huge difference to Lynda J of Mannatech. And the fix doesn't have to be a total elimination of the condition; it can also be just an improvement. Like:

> "I don't hurt like I used to anymore", or

> "Now I get colds rarely and when I do they last two days instead of a month."

Match your Befores and Afters. You can either start with a Before or with an After, whichever you remember first. It doesn't matter. What's important is that they have to match. Like:

"Before I was blind and now I can see."

Not: "Before I was blind and now I can walk." If you wanted to focus on being able to walk now, the match would be:

"Before I was lame and now I can walk."

Many people suddenly remember fixes they experienced and pile them all in on the After side of their script. Check your script so that you have matching Before problems for each of your After results, just like the weight on each side of a teeter totter.

OK?

It's time now to write down your memories. Use Box 1 below or a separate piece of paper to complete this part. Disregard the "Finale" for now. You'll be filling it in later.

BOX 1. BEFORE AND AFTER, AND YOUR FAVORITE FIX

Before #1

Before I started using the product (or service), I was someone who…

After #1

Then one day I tried this product (or service), and after _____ I noticed that
        (time period)

Finale[15]:

---

[15] Coming in a bit.

Before #2

Before I started using the product (or service), I was someone who...

After #2

Then one day I tried this product (or service), and after _____ I noticed that
(time period)

Finale[16]:

---

[16] Coming in a bit.

Before #3

Before I started using the product (or service), I was someone who...

After #3

Then one day I tried this product (or service), and after _____ I noticed that...
(time period)

Finale[17]:

---

[17] Coming in a bit.

STEP 3. Your Favorite Fix

What is the problem or concern that your product or service fixed that you are happiest about? Look at the three Afters you wrote above. As you look at each one, become aware of how each one makes you feel. Choose the one that gives you the broadest smile, the one that makes you feel the happiest or most relieved inside.

It doesn't have to be dramatic; but it has to be something YOU feel strongly about.

Circle it with a big fat red pen or with a highlighter in your favorite color. This is your Favorite Fix. This is what you'll use on your first date.

You'll have other opportunities to present others. Just not now. You may market many fixes, but you LEAD WITH ONLY ONE. Otherwise, that precious one-in-ten who's waiting may never hear you calling their name. It's the same thing Macy's does.

Remember Macy's White Sale, which they hold every summer. Ads in the newspapers scream "Macy's White Sale". How many women go to buy linens but come out of the store with things that are not white? [18]

Here's an example of what Linda L of Reliv International remembered, and what she chose as her Favorite Fix:

1) Before, she was taking 11 medications with worrisome side effects, and now she's down to 4 meds. She saved $6,000 and avoided those side effects.

2) Before, she had a life long pattern of four to five long lasting colds and coughing attacks per year. Now, she gets only a couple of normal colds per year which last one week instead of six.

3) Before, she used to have to sleep 14-18 hours a day. Now she sleeps a normal 8 and has gained 6 to 10 productive hours in the day.

---

[18] You can switch to a different fix AFTER you get your first 100 customers for the first fix, then you can lead with a different fix the next month. Many of you won't have to switch at all, especially if you have more business than you can handle with your Favorite Fix. Many people become well known specialists in their Favorite Fix and get referrals as the word gets out.

She picked her second fix. It made her feel like "a brand new person."

Here's Claire M. of Cell Tech:

1) Before, she had to take a nap every afternoon and was in bed by 8. Now she doesn't need a nap anymore and bedtime is 10-11 pm.

2) Before, she was someone who got sick a lot with a stuffy nose, headache, itchy eyes and sore throats. Now she hardly ever gets a headache.

3) Before, she had to eat every two hours, otherwise she'd get weak and feel like biting people's heads off. Now she goes much longer without having to eat and her husband and closest friends have told her how much nicer a person she is.

She picked her third fix. Claire said that because of it, she liked herself better too.

Finale

Some people feel strongly about their results because they were life altering for themselves or their families. In some cases long-term health problems were reversed.

George A of Oasis Wellness could hardly get out of bed and on his days off all he could do was sit on the floor and watch TV. In less than a month of using his product, he was able to get out of bed with lots of energy and spend time doing things with his friends. He said, "In five years I've never looked back." That's his Finale.

Steven S of Mannatech didn't have the energy to play with his grandchildren when they came to visit him because of the many medications he was taking. In a couple of months of using his product, he could pick up his grandson and hug him again. He's been free of all prescription drugs for three years. His finale: "I feel better than I've felt in 20 years."

Other finales:

"It feels good to use a product that actually makes a difference." (from someone who used to take lots of supplements and couldn't tell whether or not they were working.)

"It's been eight years and I feel better now than I ever did."

"It's been six years and they [flus] have never come back."

"It's been eight years now and I don't hurt anymore after doing the things I love."

If you have a similar feeling about your product or service, **include a finale in the After part of your Favorite Fix**. This is not necessary if you don't feel it. Don't force it or it will sound insincere, like seller talk.

<u>**From now on, all steps and instructions will refer to your Favorite Fix only**</u>.

STEP 4. Personal Zingers

These are juicy tidbits from your personal situation before you started using your product or service.

One kind of Personal Zinger includes **crises, frailties or problems that you've overcome by using your product**. Admitting that you're not perfect is endearing to others and creates a bond because you are suddenly one of them.

For example, Jodi G of Ideal Health, who had become depressed and had lost her zest for life said: "Seven years ago my relationship fell apart, and after the break up, a lot of things went downhill. After a while I stopped doing things socially and I didn't enjoy my work. Actually I didn't enjoy anything anymore. When I was in a roomful of people, I'd get anxiety attacks…" It was very difficult for her to say these things, especially in class, but she had the courage to stick with it, and consequently, she created a stellar script.

Or, Darlynn M of Mannatech, who had a lot of back problems said: "I couldn't pick up my kids to hug them or play with them, and I couldn't walk on the beach or in the mountains anymore…"

Or Pete B of Quixtar who hates to go shopping said: "I used to have to go with my wife who wants to look in every store and I just want to buy what I went there to buy…"

Or Janet P of Excel Communications who wanted to be sure she was paying the same per minute without having to check the bill each month, said: "I got so mad because I'd have to be hours on hold with my old phone company waiting to talk to someone to explain why some calls were charged at 15 cents when all calls were supposed to be 5 cents…"

Another kind of zinger if you didn't have a problem you overcame, but wanted to maintain an already good condition or ensure peak performance, is **what you've done to prove you're a member of the Segment.**

For example, Jett of Mannatech, whose market segment is people who "have always been interested in their health, in eating right, and in hitting their peak performance," said: "I've done vegetarian and I've always done supplements because I've always wanted to maintain great health and improve my athletic performance. I play sports to win, not just for exercise."

Now, it's your turn. Look at what you wrote in the **Before part of your Favorite Fix** (Box 1 above), and see if it includes a juicy tidbit or two about you. If not, add them to that part now.

STEP 5. Other Things You Tried

Thinking about those juicy tidbits, did you try to fix that situation before you came across your product?

Some people try for years to fix a problem, with little success. They try one service after another, or go from doctor to doctor, or try all kinds of vitamins, medications or alternative approaches.

Here are examples of things that some of my students tried:

> "I was on four medications that weren't helping me much and had bad side effects."

> "I tried all kinds of vitamins from our local GNC over a couple of years and it didn't seem to make a difference whether I took them or not."

> "The doctors had given up on me and I thought I'd have to be like that for the rest of my life."

> ➤ "I changed my diet and started exercising, but neither seemed to make much difference."

> ➤ If you tried things before you found your product, describe that in Box 2 below.

> ➤ Phrases that work well after saying what you tried before you found your product include:

> ➤ " … but nothing seemed to make a difference

> ➤ " … but nothing seemed to work."

> ➤ " … but they had bad side effects (and I got scared).

> ➤ " … but something was still missing."

> ➤ "I knew I'd better do something before it's too late."

> ➤ "They worked for a while, but [the problem] didn't go away."

It's better to use "Nothing SEEMED TO work (or make a difference)" instead of saying "Nothing worked (or made a difference)" because you really don't know what was going on inside your body. If you used "seemed to…," you'll come across as a careful person.

IF YOU DIDN'T TRY ANYTHING BEFORE
USING YOUR PRODUCT,
LEAVE THIS BOX BLANK.

BOX 2

Things I Tried (optional)

but nothing seemed to make a difference.
(or a similar appropriate phrase.)

Congratulations! You've completed the Remembering part. You can now come out of your Remembering Room and be back at your desk to do Scripting…

Scripting Your Market Segment

WARNING!

If you have not yet done the *Remembering* steps

and you plan to create a script,

go back to your *Remembering Room* now

and do the 3 *Remembering* steps before going any further.

---

*e*veryone in my classes, without exception, who didn't do the Remembering steps in the previous section (usually because the Scripting looked so easy), ended up with dreaded seller talk -- no matter how experienced or bright they were and despite having made the Second Agreement with themselves.

Why? Because the moment they imagined talking to a prospect, their brain automatically thought about what they should say to impress the other person. Then they started making up things they thought would turn that person on. They'd use general and fluffy words that totally lacked the authenticity and intimacy that turn consumers on.

Everyone in the class heard the fluff in seconds and sent the person right back to the Remembering Room. So, if you haven't done your Remembering, go back to your Remembering Room and do it now, so someone doesn't send you back later. Or worse, glazes over when you start talking.

Congratulations! You are now ready to start creating the first part of your First Date Script – your Market Segment.

Your Market Segment is your marketing name. It's your Favorite Fix – the juiciest problem, condition or personal goal you had, that your product or service fixed or helped you attain. It's the name you've chosen to call out – your hot button. It causes the one-in-ten to perk up their ears because they have the same hot button name and they heard you call it.

For example, Janice H of Mannatech is marketing a product that helped her get her motivation back. She could barely get out of bed and didn't even shower some days. After six months of taking her product, she started getting her motivation back, and now, after about a year she jumps out of bed and gets out of the house again like a regular person. Her market segment for her First Date Script is:

"people who have lost their motivation

 and can't seem to get it back"

Becca F of Melaleuca was energetic most of her life until she had her second baby. Then she had to lie down everyday for three hours and couldn't get anything done. Within a month of taking her product she was waking up before the alarm and didn't have to take her usual 3-hour nap. Her market segment is:

"women who were energetic

most of their lives until they

had children"

How many people do you think have the same 'name' as Janice? How about Becca? Do you think there might be 100 or 300 or 1000 people for each of them out there? …

How to Find Your Personal Market Segment

Go to your Favorite Fix in Box 1 of the Remembering section. It's the one you circled or highlighted. Look at what you wrote in the corresponding "Before" part.

Convert that Before into your Personal Market Segment by using it or a version of it to complete any one of these sentences, whichever is most appropriate:

I market a product for someone who…

I market a product for people who…

I market a product for women who…

I market a product for men who…

I market a product for parents who…

For example, Claire M's Favorite Fix was that she can go longer without eating, and she's now a much nicer person, according to her husband and closest friends. Her "Before" for that fix was "Before I started taking the product I was someone who had to eat every couple of hours, otherwise I'd get weak and feel like biting people's heads off."

To get her Personal Market Segment, she completed the sentence:

I market a product for someone who…

with:

"can't go for more than a couple of hours without eating."

So, her market segment is:

people who can't go for more than a couple of hours without eating

Ernie H of Mannatech, was someone who had trouble sleeping and got big flus often as a consequence. Within a month of taking his product, he could sleep like a normal person again and no longer got big flus from lack of rest. His market segment is:

people who have trouble sleeping

Don't lapse into techno-babble or naming diseases. Ernie H doesn't say "people who have insomnia", he says "people who have trouble sleeping".

Instead of "fibromyalgia" one says "people whose muscles ache all the time and can't get up in the morning."

To come up with the picture words that describe symptoms, ask yourself:

"What did that feel like?"

"How did I know I had that condition?"

or say to yourself:

"What I mean is….", for example "I had insomnia. What I mean is I had trouble sleeping."

The questions above also work to make vague words like "tired" or "no energy", or "depressed" more specific.

When Janice H said she suffered from "depression", I asked her:

> **"What do you mean? How did you know you were depressed?"**

Among other things, she said:

"I lost my motivation…"

Bingo!

She markets a product for people who *have lost their motivation and can't seem to get it back.*

Sometimes you'll need to dig deeper to find the key condition, or the trigger that resulted in the problems your product fixed.

For example, when a student said she used to fall asleep babysitting her grandchildren,

I asked her what caused that to happen.

She said:

"All the medication I was taking made me feel really tired and out of it."

Bingo! She says:

"I market a product for *someone who is tired and out of it because they take lots of medication.*"

And

"falling asleep babysitting their grand-children"

became a personal zinger that followed the market segment in her script .

The questions you can ask yourself to dig more deeply include:

"Why did I feel like that?"

"What caused that to happen?" or

"What happened just before I felt like that?"

Here are a few more Personal Market Segments that we created for students in the Three Scripts classes, based on their Before situations, Personal Zingers, and triggers that emerged as we worked on the scripts in class:

> People who have become depressed and lost their zest for life

> People who know they're not eating right and are interested in health

> People who have always had an interest in health, in eating right and in hitting their peak performance

> People who were healthy all their lives and suddenly got diagnosed with a life-threatening disease

> People who compete in sports and are frustrated because they are feeling the pains of getting older.

> People who can't seem to lose weight with diet, exercise or will power

> People who hate to go shopping

> People who never thought they could afford to have a lawyer at their beck and call

> Women who have a lot of trouble during that time of the month

> Women who want a natural alternative to the hormone replacement drugs they're taking

> People whose joints hurt a lot

> Parents with kids who have allergies

> Parents with kids who don't eat right

IF MY PRODUCT'S SO GREAT, HOW COME I CAN'T SELL IT?

> Parents who want to do everything they can to raise healthy kids

> People who have big phone bills and worry about what their phone bill is going to be every month

> People who want to get rid of their credit card debt

At the end of your market segment add a 'like me' phrase or something similar:

like me

like I used to be

like what happened to me

like I did

This tells the consumer that you are a member of that market segment, and most important, it shows the person that you have vulnerabilities also. That revelation seems to hold the person's attention and it somehow endears you to them. It's the opposite of sounding like a bossy know-it-all to whom no one wants to listen. And it allows you to segue from the market segment to your personal zingers.

For example, Xi C of Nu Skin says:

> "I market a product for people who have
> dull dry skin and wrinkles, LIKE I USED
> TO. Since I was little, my skin was dry,
> like my Mom's. I spent a lot of time
> outdoors in the sun and my skin got
> worse. It started flaking and I got a lot of
> deep wrinkles around my eyes...

Sometimes it's easier to decide which personal
tidbits meant the most to you, then work
backwards to the market segment. Up to you.

OK, here's the box for you to write in your
market segment. Imagine someone you just met asks
you: "What do you do?" You reply:

BOX 3

My Market Segment

I market a product for someone (or people, or women, or men, or parents) who...

...like me / ...like I used to be / ...like what happened to me / ...like I did

---

Many congratulations! You have finished building the foundation for your First Date Script. What's left is to put it together and do a final polish to make it zing...

Assembling Your First Date Script

Remember Einstein's formula $e = mc^2$? With that formula he shifted the paradigm that had formed the basis for Western science for centuries. It went from Newton's mechanistic laws to Einstein's laws of relativity.

This chapter lays out the formula I have used to help over 1,500 students create First Date Scripts. It may not be as earth shaking as Einstein's, but what if it changes the results of your marketing efforts? And what if it changes the way you feel about doing your business? How about changing the way other people see you? Or the way you feel about yourself?

Here's what a few students have written me, after using the scripts we derived in class from this formula.

"I don't have to pretend I'm someone I'm not, anymore."

- Bobbi M, Shaklee

"I have my confidence back."
— Jan H, Melaleuca

"After 37 years, I finally know what to say to my old friends."

— Mary A, Shaklee

"It's fun again."

— Janet O, Shaklee

"They treat me like a normal person now. What a relief."

— Cynthia H, Tahitian Noni

"I feel as excited as I did nine years ago..."

— Bonnie B, Mannatech

"It's like a paradigm shift…"

-- Maggie B, Mannatech

Six weeks after Bob Ferguson and his mother Kay Ferguson's Shaklee downline started using their First Date and follow-up scripts in customer campaigns, Bob called me up at two o'clock one morning to say:

"Kim, I just looked at my volume this month and had to call you. My volume for the first two weeks of the month went up 35% and December is our slow season! I know that most of it is because of your Three Scripts class. We're running a holiday special, but the increases are coming from people who have taken your class and are going to your Study Halls... Thank you. Thank you."

The First Date Script has five Personal Pieces that come out of your personal experience. You created them in the previous chapters.

1) Market segment (Box 3)

2) Personal zingers (Box 1 – Before)

3) Things you tried, to fix your problem or concern (Box 2)

4) Your results after using your product or service (Box 1 – After)

5) Your optional Finale (Box 1)

The First Date Script also has certain 'Key Phrases' that introduce or end each piece. These phrases open the mind of a consumer. They are the result of thousands of selling conversations I've had over many years of direct marketing. This phrasing worked the best and the most consistently for me, and now, is working consistently for a growing number of Three Scripts graduates who are using the scripts in many different kinds of situations.

OK. Here comes the formula. The Key Phrases are in bold italics. The Personal Pieces are marked with a "+".

BOX 4.

First Date Scripting Formula

I market[19] a product[20] for someone[21] who...

> \+ Personal Your Market Segment (Box 3)

...like what happened to me[22].

> \+ Your Personal Zingers (Box 1 – the Before part of your Favorite Fix)
>
> \+ Things You Tried (Box 2 - optional)

but nothing seemed to make a difference (or other appropriate phrase.)
So then I tried this product and after ____months[23]

> \+ Your Results (Box 1 – the After part of your Favorite Fix)
>
> \+ Finale (Box 1 – end of the After part of your Favorite Fix - optional)

Do you know anyone who might like to know about a product[24] like that?

---

[19] or "I'm introducing…"

[20] or "service"

[21] or "people" or "women" or "men" or "parents" or other appropriate group

[22] or "like me" or "like I used to", or "like I did", or similar phrase.

[23] Use "within a month" if your results happened right away, so that you don't sound like a seller who's exaggerating, even if you had immediate results.

[24] or "service"

Here are three examples of the completed formula. These are First Date Scripts being used by graduates of the Three Scripts class, who have reported activity and results way beyond their previous experience.

SAMPLE SCRIPT 1
Jim M, Ideal Health

OPENER	**I market a product**
MARKET SEGMENT: WHO	**for people who**
PERSONAL MARKET SEGMENT	run a demanding business and have lost their energy,
LIKE ME	**like what happened to me**.
PERSONAL ZINGERS	I ran a medical practice for 25 years, and during the last four years, when the government got involved, I lost my freedom to run it. I worked longer hours, did more procedures, saw my family less and made less money. I'd come home after work with no

energy. I'd fall asleep on the couch within 10 minutes after dinner. I was so wiped out that my family stopped including me in their evening plans. They said "Dad's no fun". Even my dog and cat didn't want to be with me. So I had to do something about it.

THINGS TRIED (OPT.)   I had access to prescription drugs,

TURNING POINT   **but I was looking for something natural** to boost my energy.

I TRIED   **So I tried this product,**

TIME FRAME   **and within a month,**

RESULTS   I started coming home with more energy than I had before. I didn't go to the couch any more after dinner. Instead I stayed awake and spent time with my family.

FINALE (OPTIONAL)   **It's been 4 and a half years**

and I feel like I'm in my 30s again. The best part is the kids say 'Dad's fun again'.

END QUESTION **Do you know anyone who might like to know about a product like that?**

SAMPLE SCRIPT 2
Mary A, Shaklee

OPENER **I market a product**

MARKET SEGMENT:
 WHO **for people who**

PERSONAL
MARKET SEGMENT have always had major health problems,

LIKE ME **like I had.**

PERSONAL ZINGERS I ate horribly, smoked, used alcohol, and drank coffee. When I was 26, the doctor told me I might have 10 years to go. He told me to stop all these things and get more rest. So I went cold

	turkey. That helped quite a bit, but I still wasn't really healthy, and I always had headaches and the runs.
THINGS TRIED (OPT.)	I tried a lot of health products to find something that would work.
TURNING POINT	--
I TRIED	**One day my husband got me to try a new product**
TIME FRAME (1)	**and almost immediately**
RESULTS (1)	my energy started to come back.
TIME FRAME (2)	**Within a month**
RESULTS (2)	I got rid of the headaches and the runs.
FINALE (OPTIONAL)	**It's been 30 years now, and I feel like I should have when I was 21.**
END QUESTION	**Do you know anyone who might like to know about a product like that?**

SAMPLE SCRIPT 3
Cliff W, Excel Communications

OPENER	**I market a phone service**
MARKET SEGMENT: WHO	**for people who**
PERSONAL MARKET SEGMENT	are conscious of every long distance call they make and worry about what their phone bill is going to be.
LIKE ME	**like I used to.**
PERSONAL ZINGERS	I used to dread getting the phone bill in the mail every month and was constantly changing my phone features to get a better deal.
THINGS TRIED (OPT.)	--
TURNING POINT	--
I TRIED	**Then I tried this other phone service**
TIME FRAME	**and now**

RESULTS	I've stopped diddling with the phone features trying to get a better deal, I'm no longer conscious of every long distance call I make, and I know what my phone bill is going to be every month, so I don't worry about it anymore.
FINALE (OPTIONAL)	--
END QUESTION	**Do you know anyone who might like to know about a service like that?**

The pieces of the formula

After using this formula mostly unconsciously tens of thousands of times over the last 15 years, I can tell you the significance of each piece.

OPENER. "I market a product…" tells the consumer right off that you market the product or service you're about to describe. Being up front about the fact that you're a seller preserves your credibility.

MARKET SEGMENT: WHO. The Market Segment has two parts: the 'who' phrase and the description of your Personal Market Segment. The 'who' phrase ('for someone who, or 'for people who,' etc.... tells the consumer that it's not for everyone. This keeps their attention because their mind automatically wonders whom it's for – you know, just in case.

PERSONAL MARKET SEGMENT. This is the name you have chosen to call out – it's your Favorite Fix. It causes the one-in-ten to perk up their ears because they have the same name and they heard you call it.

LIKE ME. "like me" (or other appropriate tag line) at the end of the market segment tells them that you are a member of that market segment and endears you to them. Plus it beefs up your image as an advisor with personal experience.

PERSONAL ZINGERS. This is the part that touches a consumer. It reminds them of their own pain, their own needs and problems. Or it causes them to think of someone they know who has a similar experience, and it endears you to them. Personal Zingers help you establish instant rapport even with total strangers.

THINGS YOU TRIED. This tells them that you are a knowledgeable consumer. And if they have tried the same sorts of things, they can now perhaps move the particular problem to their Change List.

TURNING POINT. **"but nothing seemed to make a difference."** explains why you were open to trying another product or service.

I TRIED. **"Then one day I tried this product"**: introduces your product

TIME FRAME. **"and after (or within) x months"**: gives them facts about your results. A word of caution: If you experienced results in a few days or some short period less than a month, say "within a few weeks" or "almost right away" in your script. Even if you rose from the dead in a day. Otherwise, you run the risk of not being believable and sounding like a seller bear.

RESULTS. Your results, including your Finale, tells them about the benefits they can picture in their own minds. What happened to you may trigger visions in their mind about what might happen to them if they used your product. You're describing benefits without making any promises you can't keep.

END QUESTION. "Do you know anyone who might like to know about a product like that?" This is your "Close". It puts no pressure on a consumer because you're not asking them to buy. You're simply asking if they know anyone who might like to know about a product like that. If you've hit their hot button, they'll have the pleasure of saying, "Yes, me! I want to know more." If not, but they know someone who fits the bill, they may think of them and give you a referral. If it's not their name or that of anyone they know, you've simply "called the wrong number."

OK. It's your turn now.

Have the First Date Scripting Formula (Box 4 a few pages back) in front of you as a guide when you write the first draft of your script in Box 5 on the next page.

Don't give in to the temptation of copying verbatim a sample script that's similar to your situation. You can take it as a model, but give it your personal twist. Students have always marveled at how many different scripts emerged from people who were marketing the same product. No two were ever the same.

Your personal twist is what will cause you to sound like a consumer rather than a seller bear. And many of my students have reported that they really enjoyed using it because it felt so comfortable. Discover your truth, so you can have a script that you love madly!

BOX 5

My First Date Script: First Draft

(Use formula in Box 3 above)

Tips to Make Your Script Zing

Certain types of words and phrases touch people and open their minds, while others cause eyes to glaze and minds to close. Here are some things you can do to catch the attention of those one-in-tens.

1.   **Use words a 13-year old would understand.** For adults, this is more easily said than done. Here are some tricks to help.

SAY your script OUT LOUD. One part at a time. Your ears MUST hear it to judge it. Written language is very different from spoken language, and tends to be duller, stiffer, and more formal. SPEAK YOUR SCRIPT for your consumer ears.

If possible, have someone else there to listen, so they can tell you if that's the way you'd say that to a 13-year old.

If you have no one, stand in front of the mirror and say your script.

If you cannot judge on hearing it if you'd say it to a 13 year-old or not, RECORD YOURSELF and play it back.

Say it again and again, better and better, until you KNOW that's what you'd say to a 13 year old at the kitchen table, or to an old friend while sipping lattes.

2. Make sure there's **no seller talk** in your script. Make sure it's speaking to someone, there's no techno-babble and no promises, chestbeating or screaming. See Chapter 4 to refresh your memory.

3. **Use picture and action words.** NO clichés or generalities that speak to no one in particular and which put the listener in the doze zone, or cause their eyes to glaze over. Big words, use of the passive voice, and droning on and on tend to do that. Replace each cliché or boring generality with picture or action words.

Generalities	Picture words or action words
I was so tired…	I had to lie down on the couch after dinner each night
I didn't feel good…	I snapped at my children and nobody liked that.

I couldn't do anything.

I used to run everyday and now I couldn't.

I was sick and tired of being sick and tired.

I couldn't dance and play tennis anymore like I used to every week.

Disease	How you felt or what you had to do or couldn't do
I had fibromyalgia.	I ached all over and I couldn't get up in the morning.
I had arthritis	My feet and legs hurt so much I couldn't sleep.
My wife had Alzheimer's	My wife couldn't remember what she had just said or where she had put her keys. It got so bad she got lost a block from home.
Chronic fatigue	I had to lie down several times during the day. I was so weak, sometimes I could barely climb up the stairs.
Asthma	I couldn't breathe. I was sniffling

	and wheezing all the time and couldn't go out without my inhaler.
ADHD	My son had ADHD. He couldn't sleep more than 4 to 5 hours a night. He wet the bed 3 times a week, and couldn't sit still or pay attention.

OK?

Now you may want to **go over the first draft of your First Date Script in Box 5 and give it a polish**..

Finally, **time your polished script**. Make sure it is no more than 45 seconds – max.

Box 6 below is for your <u>final</u> First Date Script. **Congratulations!**

BOX 6 MY FIRST DATE SCRIPT: FINAL

My First Date Script: Final

Short First Date Script:
Your Personal Market Segment Script

Depending on the situation, you can use either your full First Date Script (which we've been calling just 'First Date Script' (abbreviated 'FDS') or a short version of it. Some people call it their 'Personal Market Segment Script,' because it consists mostly of just their personal market segment.

Here's Jim's Short FDS. His FDS is the first sample script a few pages back. If you turn back to it now, you'll see how we just pulled out the first four pieces of his FDS and tacked on the End Question.

OPENER	**I market a product**
MARKET SEGMENT: WHO	**for people who**
PERSONAL MARKET SEGMENT	**run a demanding business and have lost their energy,**
LIKE ME	**like what happened to me**.

END QUESTION **Do you know anyone who might like to know about a product like that?**

You can **use the short FDS in situations where you're making fast cold calls, or only have 15 seconds** in the store or in line at Kinko's to answer a quick "So what do you do?"

You'll add your Personal Zingers later, if there's interest, when you do Script 2b coming up in the next chapter. Script 2b lays out how to slide your Personal Zingers in the conversation that follows your FDS, after your one-in-ten shows interest in your fix.

Limit your Personal Market Segment to 19 words or less. You're giving only your 'name', not your story. To see if the other person has that 'name' as one of theirs – the details come after they go "Yeah, that sounds like me…"

Here's the formula for your Personal Market Segment Script. Use it to write your Personal Market Segment Script in Box 9 following.

BOX 8

Personal Market Segment Script Formula
(<u>Short</u> First Date Script)

I market[25] a product[26] for someone[27] who...

+ Personal Market Segment (Box 3)

...like what happened to me[28].

Do you know anyone who might like to know about a product[29] like that?

---

[25] or "I'm introducing…" or "My company's introducing…"

[26] or "service"

[27] or "people" or "women" or "men" or "parents" or other appropriate group

[28] or "like me" or "like I used to", or "like I did", or similar phrase.

[29] or "service"

BOX 9

<u>Short</u> First Date Script

Good work. Now, close your eyes, take a deep, relaxing breath and make the Third Agreement with yourself...

Third Agreement

Lead with
YOUR
hot button

Close your eyes and say it out loud, with all your heart.

When Someone Says Yes:
Scripts 1, 2 and 3

Once someone hears you call their hot button or that of someone they know, they respond to see what you might have for them. Then the Seller-Consumer dance begins.

There are three points in the verbal dance when what you say either keeps them tuned in or they start to change the channel. It's when they ask:

> **What is it?**

> **Will it work for me?**   Will it work for Uncle Harry? Will it work for problem X? and

> **How much is it?**

What you say then will tell them whether you're an advisor they can trust or whether you're just another seller type.

Follow-Up Scripts 1, 2, and 3 illustrate how an Advisor might answer these pivotal questions.

Script 1. 'What is it?'

A typical seller will grab this opening to launch into their product spiel, starting with the names of the product and the company. **NOT!**

An advisor-seller starts with a phrase describing briefly the nature of the product, then mentions the product name. Not the company name. Why load the consumer's mind with techno-babble when you want them to focus on the hot button you and they have in common? Here's how an advisor might answer this question:

> ➢ "It's liquid vitamins. It's called Liquamin, have you heard of it?"

Or instead of 'liquid vitamins':

> ➢ "nontoxic cleaners…"
>
> ➢ "fruits and veggies in capsules…"
>
> ➢ "a powder you mix with water or juice to make a shake…"
>
> ➢ "a phone service that gives you free lon distance with your local service…"

> ➤ "a delivery service for anything you buy at grocery stores, drug stores or malls…"

> ➤ "a natural skin care line from France…"

> ➤ "a soy protein drink…"

> ➤ "an air filter that doesn't make any noise…"

etc.

Here's the formula

Script 1. "What is it?"

It's (a short phrase or sentence describing the product or service. See above examples.)

It's called (name of product).
Have you heard of it?

What you say next will depend on what the consumer says. They might say:

"No I haven't heard of it. How much does it cost?"

Or,

"No, I've never heard of it. Hmmm…"

Or,

> **"No. Do you think it will work for my**
>
> **7-year old son?"**

Follow-Up Scripts 2 and 3 below describe how to respond.

Script 2. 'Will It Work for Me?'

This script has two parts – 2a, the disclaimer, and 2b, the rapport builder. 2b has two options depending on whether you lead with your complete First Date Script or with just the Short version.

Script 2a. Imagine you've just approached a consumer with your First Date Script. The consumer says:

> "Gee, that sounds like me. You
>
> think it will work for me?"

What do you think a typical seller would immediately say? …

> "Of course it will work for you!!
>
> Everyone loves it. Plus it's really cutting

edge, inspired by Nobel prize winning scientists, and it's patented. It even cleans your toilet and makes your skin smoother. Plus it's bioavailable and biodegradable ... ..."

But since you're an **advisor**, here's what you say instead:

> ### Script 2a. Disclaimer
> **"I don't know if this will work for you or not, but what if it does? What if it works for you the way it did for me? Would you like to try it then?"**

Pause. Breathe.

You know only that it has worked for you. That's all you've said. No promises. No hype. There's just one question on the table: <u>Would the consumer like to try it if it works for them the way it did for you?</u>

133

Script 2b. If you get a pause that's inquiring, or thoughtful, do this. Mentally cross over from your side of the booth and slide right in next to them on their side. Speak in a friendly tone, *like you are confiding.* The words you use depend on whether you led with just your Short First Date Script or with your full First Date Script.

If you led with your full First Date Script, pick one of the two options below, depending on why you got into the business:

1)   If you got into the business because you fell in love with the product or service when you first tried it or heard about it, here's what you say.

Script 2b-1. Product Motive
(For After First Date Script)

"Let me tell you what happened to me.

I liked the product so much I decided to go into business for myself and make it available to other people like me. So they can try it too. And that's what I'm doing.[30] So, what do you think? Would you like to try this out and see if it works for you (the way it did for me)?"

---

2)　　　If you got into the business not because you experienced any great effects from the products, but because you were looking for a business to get involved in, then, you'd use the following script instead

---

[30] If you prefer, use "market it" or "sell it" instead of "make it available". If you are taking their money, "share" is out. If you're giving it away, "share" is in.

Script 2b-2. Business Motive
(For After First Date Script)

"Let me tell you what happened to me.

I'd been looking to represent a company that had a product I could really get behind. I found it in this one, so that's what I'm doing.[31] So what do you think? Would you like to try it and see if it works for you (the way it did for me)?"

If you use the Short First Date Script, and the person asks you "Will it work for me?" or "Does it really work?" this is your chance to slide in your personal zingers and results. Script 2c shows how you'd do it.

---

[31] If you prefer, use "market it" or "sell it" instead of "make it available." If you are taking their money, "share" is out. If you're giving it away, "share" is in.

Script 2c. Personal Zingers
(For After Short First Date Script)

"Let me tell you what happened to me.

Before I heard about this product (or service),

I used to be someone who...(your Personal

Zingers, the Things You Tried, and your Results

from your First Date Script). **In fact,**

Option 1): I liked the product so much I

decided to go into business for myself and

make it available to other people like me.

Option 2): I'd been looking to represent a

company that had a product I could really get

behind, and I found it in this one.

And that's what I'm doing.[32] So, what do you

think? Would you like try this out and see if it

works for you (the way it did for me)?"

---

[32] If you prefer, use "market it" or "sell it" instead of "make it available." If you are taking their money, "share" it out. If you're giving it away, "share" is in.

Pause. *Breathe.* Go with the flow as it comes from the consumer.

Notice that you dropped the hint about "the business" in that last piece of script. A HINT. That's it. If they have even the slightest interest in doing the business they'll catch the hint. Respect their intelligence and level of curiosity and don't say any more. If they're curious, they'll ask.

Your ONLY focus right now is seeing if they might be right as a regular customer. OK? Have you ever lost a customer by pressing them to do the business at this very moment? ... (More on this coming up.)

They will react to 2b in one of three ways. They will either:

1) Waffle or get pukey on you;

2) Ask you for more information; or

3) Ask you how much it costs.

If they waffle or get pukey on you: Immediately **say *No* first**: "This is probably not for you..." I've given you a number of ways to say *No* first in previous books and audiotapes.[33] These techniques helped me preserve my self-esteem when I came across the thousands of people who were not the right ones for my business or product.

If they ask you for more information, ask them how they'd like it: By email or website? A conference call? A get-together? Or by snail mail? Make a date to talk more another time, or to get more info to them IF you think they're worth your time.

Remember that many people don't know how to say, "No, this is not for me." So, they ask you to mail them information just to be nice and get you off the phone. If that happens, here's what I used to say:

---

[33] In my book *Rules for the New New MLMer* (2001) and my audiotapes *So You Want to Be a Networker* and *How To Build a Giant Heap with or without Your Friends, Family or Neighbors*.
See http://WhoWho911.com/store.

Script 2d. More Info

"OK I can send you some info and I'll call you in a few days to see if there's a match. Otherwise, if you're not really interested it's OK. We can save a tree and I won't burst into tears, I promise. So what would you like to do? Shall I send you some information and I'll call you in a couple of days? Or do you want to save a tree?"

If they ask how much it costs, go into Script 3, coming up.

SCRIPT 3. 'How much is it?'

This is the biggie. Hearing it often makes marketers nervous, because they know that this is the moment of truth. They'll either be up one customer, or they'll lose them.

Here's how to be totally ready for this question, perhaps even to look forward to it.

First, remind yourself that you really are an advisor. If your product is right for them, they'll buy at some point and you'll be ecstatic. If it's not, at least you'll have done your job of letting them know about it. You can lead a horse to water, but…

Second, prepare in advance what you'll say, so that when the moment comes, it will roll off your tongue and you'll enjoy the conversation.

Your response to the question has four parts. Therefore, Script 3 has four parts:

3a.   Packages

3b.   What you did

3c.   Your surprise advice

3d.   Special pricing options

3a. Packages

"Packages" are the different ways a consumer can get what you're offering. For example, at the local coffee house, they offer three sizes – large, medium and small. They're the same quality stuff, from the same pot, but one has more of it than the other. Depends on what you're in the mood for.

Same when someone buys a TV or computer. Dell customizes any computer for anyone's needs. Some are bigger and have more bells and whistles, some are smaller or are just different. They're all Dell quality.

Customers like to see their options from the get-go, don't you? Offering options awakens their perception of you as an advisor, rather than a seller with an agenda of their own.

The packages you offer must relate to the market segment you described to the consumer. For example, if your market segment is people who have achy joints, your packages must address that concern. The small package might offer a cream to rub on the joints plus an herbal pill to decrease the inflammation. The large package may, in addition, contain general nutritional support, like a multi vitamin and a multi mineral.

Three Scripts class graduates from several companies have put together packages that follow these guidelines. You can, too.

OK. Imagine a consumer has just popped the big question: "How much is it?"

Here's your Opener:

"It depends. Let me tell you how it comes."
The rest of what you say depends on whether you are marketing one product or a line of different products.

If you are marketing one product, your company probably offers price breaks based on volume. For example, if the break points are 1 bottle, 3 bottles and 12 bottles, you might say:

3a-1. Volume Breaks

It depends. Let me tell you how it comes. One bottle is normally good for a month. They give you a 1-month supply (or a bottle) for $_____, a 3-month supply (or a box of 3) for $_____, and a 12-month supply (or a case of 12) for $_____.

Optional question:

Which one do you think might be good for you?

If you are marketing a line of products, here's what you might say:

3a-2. Package Pricing

It depends. Let me tell you how it comes.

They **have a couple of packages, depending on what you want. They have a deluxe package and a starter.**[34]

* In the DELUXE package, you get BLAH BLAH BLAH, and they give it to you for $ ____ (retail price)

* In the STARTER package, you get BLAH BLAH, and they give it to you for $ ____ (retail price)

Optional question:

Which one do you think might be good for you?

Pause... Breathe...

The first phrase "Let me tell you how it comes" prepares the consumer's mind to receive the information

---

[34] You might have three options: deluxe, medium, and starter.

you are about to give them.

Using "They have" instead of "We" or "I have" separates you from your company. This is critical to maintain your advisor role. The moment you say "I have x…" the customer is reminded that you are the seller, and may become more skeptical than they need to be.

Giving the retail or 1-month price allows you to offer them a deal – a lower price for the same thing depending on the quantity or number of items they order. Every consumer loves a deal. It follows the classic rule of good marketing: Provide a contrast.

A customer's perception of whether something is expensive or reasonable is relative. Tony Robbins often told the story of the Number One seller of Girl Scout cookies. This young girl went door-to-door. She'd ask the person who came to the door if they'd like to buy a vacation trip to help the Girl Scouts – for $895. Most people looked at her in disbelief and said "Not today." She then offered a box of Girl Scout cookies for $7, and almost everyone bought, even though $7 for cookies was higher than most people paid for a box of cookies at the store at that time.

3b. How You Started

As they ponder options, you mentally cross over to their side of the booth and slide right in beside them. In a friendly, soft and confidential tone, say this:

Script 3b. How I Started

Let me tell you what I did. When I first got started,
[Pick A or B, whichever is true for you]

A

I wasn't sure about the products, you know, so I started with the smallest package. Then, when I saw how well it worked, I upgraded to the bigger one. (Describe your upgrade, e.g., "I took an additional test," or "I also got the vitamin powder."), or

B

I loved everything I saw, and got the deluxe package right off. And I've never looked back.

3c. Surprise Advice

Now, REGARDLESS OF WHICH OPTION YOU PICKED, go ahead and surprise your prospect. Propose this right after you tell what you did.

Script 3c. Advice

Maybe the starter package is the best one for you. Tell me how you would use the product and we can see if that's the best option ... (Ask advisor questions. See below.)

Your consumer is no dummy. What do you think they expect a seller to recommend – the biggest or the smallest? ...

What would an advisor suggest? ...

By recommending the Starter package first, you have just shown that you do not have a hidden agenda. That it's OK for them to start small, no matter what you did or what you wish they would do. Any consumer knows you wish they'd buy the big package. That's why when you don't suggest the deluxe package, the surprise is so pleasant for them.

My students have reported that customers often sigh with relief and go, "Ahh, yes, that's what I was thinking, the Starter package."

If you perceive that the consumer is ready to buy, go on to 3d.

However, if you see that they're still "thinking", don't stop there. Act like an advisor and find out a little about your customer before you ask for the sale. Here are some questions to help you advise them better and to help your customer decide on the best package for them. Select which are appropriate for what you're offering.

> How many people in the family are there?
> How big is the house you're cleaning?
> Do you need some for the beach house?
> How often will you be using it?
> Do you need a double dose?

As you get to know the customer a little better, and they tell you the problems they're looking to fix, ask more specific advisory questions. Choose what's appropriate.

> How long have you had this situation? / How long have you felt like this? How long have you been concerned about that?

> What kinds of things have you done about it [to try and fix it] so far?

> How did that work?

> What other kinds of problems would you like to test for?

> What other kinds of problems would you like to deal with?

Advisory questions for people marketing services such as long distance, legal or Internet programs:

> What are you doing for phone service now?

> How much is your phone bill now?

> Where do you call long distance? Mostly in the US or international?

> What sorts of legal help are you looking for?

A will?   Help fixing tickets?   Or a divorce?

> How often in the last couple of years have you wished you had an attorney?

> How much do you use the Internet?

> How much email do you use? Do you do video conferencing?

These are examples of information gathering questions. After you hear the answer, then you and the consumer can both decide if the starter package is still best, or if they'd like to order more things. Long distance or legal service companies usually have preset monthly programs already available. If not, you can create your own. For long distance programs, make sure the person is spending enough right now so that you can offer them a better deal. If you can't, they're not a one-in-ten for you.

REMEMBER: Before asking these questions, ALWAYS recommend the starter package first. One, to put them at ease. Two, to help them perceive you as an advisor, not just a seller.

And remember: **Before** you answer any of their questions, ask yourself, "What would an advisor say *now*?" Then speak. You may find that you catch yourself lots of times all ready to go with the old seller talk. Stop yourself and take on the role of advisor.

It could be fun...

3d. Special Pricing Options

Many companies have different pricing available for the same products. They fall into two basic categories: the 'wholesale/member pricing' and the 'autoship/preferred customer/quantity pricing'.

Say the consumer selects the Starter package. Here's what you can say to introduce the Wholesale/Member option:

3d-1. Wholesale Member Price

OK great. The price I gave you was retail. That's what they give it to you for when you're not a member. They also have a wholesale member option. Here's how that works.

You know how Sam's Club and Costco have an annual membership for about $45/year. And then you get things at a special member price? This works like that. They give you an annual membership for $____, and then you get this Starter (or whichever package they chose) for $___ instead of $___. And during the next year, you get all the products at ___% off – because you're a member. That's what I do, to get the better price. Would you like to do that too for the special price, or would you like to do retail?

Students in my classes have asked why they should offer the one-time retail options, since it's just a one-time sale. Others have asked why they shouldn't offer just the retail option first so that they can make more money on that first sale. You offer TWO options because you are an Advisor, and that's what advisors do – offer a minimum of two options. Here's a pricing option. The one that will set you up to receive that monthly income we talked about at the beginning of this book. Expect this to take a few dates, just like it would for you if you were in your consumer shoes. You don't make a big commitment after the first date, do you? …

If they are leaning towards a shorter commitment, you might say:

> **"give yourself a minimum of three months on the product, to give it a chance to work."**

Script 3d-2.
Autoship/Preferred Customer/Quantity Price

OK great. The price I gave you was retail. But you know how things are cheaper by the dozen, right? Well this works like that.

<u>Option A</u>:

You don't have to buy a dozen at once to get the preferred customer price of $____ instead of $____. They let you get it each month over ____months (check your company customer plan) and they still give you the preferred customer price because you commit to getting it each month. And they'll ship it to you direct so you don't have to do anything else. That's what I do, too, to get the better price.[35]

<u>Option B</u>:

A 1-month supply is $39.95 and a 3-month is $100 and a 12-month supply is $300.

So which one do you want to do? Do you want to do one month for $____ or do 3 months (or 12) for $____?

---

[35] Do not bring up any cancellation policy. Of course, if they ask, say: "Of course they let you cancel if you don't love it madly."

Despite all your good words, expect that some people will opt for the one-time or smallest purchase, even if it's a bit more. It's OK. They're being cautious; they want to try it first. When they start feeling its effects, they usually upgrade if it's a hot button for them, too.

So let people get on the product or service to try it for a few months, to show them that the stuff works. Then follow up without nagging, to see how it's working, and to be there when they're ready to make a longer commitment.

When I marketed the fruits and veggies in capsules, we'd say "They come in a four-month supply for you to try them." And that's what most people did. They bought the four-month supply. I didn't offer a one-month supply because I believed someone had to use it for at least three months to notice a difference or to feel more confident that they were doing the right thing for themselves.

Many other nutritional products work that way. I wanted customers who realized that nutritional supplements take time to work to rebuild the body. They're not a quick fix like drugs or surgery, which do not usually rebuild.

Let's put it all together now, so you can see how it flows in a real conversation.

Sample Conversation with That One-in-Ten

Scene:

Potential consumer and seller meet up. After the usual niceties:

CONSUMER 1

So what do you do?

YOU

I market a product for people who work long hours and are so tired when they get home, they can't do anything, **like what happened to me.**

Do you know anyone who might like to know about a product like that?

CONSUMER

Hmm. Interesting. That sounds kind of like me. What is it?

YOU

It's liquid vitamins. You take a capful once or twice a day. It's called Liquamin. Have you heard of it?

(Pause... Breathe...)

CONSUMER

No. Hmmm ...

YOU

(in a confiding tone)

Let me tell you what happened to me. I used to run a day care center for years. Before I heard about this product I used to be so tired when I got home at night I couldn't do anything else, like my gardening and needlework, and my husband got really lonesome.

Then after a month on this product, my energy started to come back. I could stay awake at the end of the day, and spend time with my husband. (Pause.)

I liked the product so much I decided to go into business for myself and market it to other people like me. And that's what I'm doing.[36] So, what do you think? **Would you like try it out and see if it works for you** (the way it did for me)?"

CONSUMER

How much does it cost? ...

YOU

It depends. Let me tell you how it comes. *They* have a couple of packages, depending on what you want. They have a deluxe package and a starter. In the Deluxe package you get blah blah blah and they give it to you for $249. In the Starter package, you get blah blah, and they give it to you for $99.

CONSUMER

Hmm. That sounds good. I wonder what I should do?

---

[36] Use "market" or "make it available to others" if you prefer, to "sell". If you are taking their money, "share" is out. If you're giving it away, "share" is in.

YOU

Let me tell you what I did. When I first got started, I wasn't sure about the products, you know, so I started with the smallest package. Then, when I saw how well it worked, I upgraded to the bigger one. Maybe the starter package is the best one for you. Tell me how you would use it and we can see if that's the best option. Are you the only one who's going to be using it? Or is your husband going to use it too?

CONSUMER

It's just me. So I'd like to get the starter package.

YOU

OK great. The price I gave you was retail. But you know how things are cheaper by the dozen, right? Well this works like that. Except you don't have to buy a dozen at once to get the preferred customer price. They let you get it each month over the next 6 months and they still give you the preferred customer price because you commit to getting it each month. And they ship it to you direct so you don't have to do anything else to get it. That's what I do to get the better price. (And of course, they let you cancel the program if you don't love it madly.)

So which one do you want to do? Do you want to be a preferred customer for $79 or do the retail for $99?

> **CONSUMER**
>
> I want to be a preferred customer.

YOU

OK great. So which credit card do you want to use?... ☺

Should I Tell Them about the Business?

Have you ever tried telling a customer about the business when they're ready to buy the product or service? ... What happened? ... Hmmm.

You just got a precious customer. How about you just congratulate yourself and make the next call?

You may not realize it, but asking a prospective customer to sell the thing they are just deciding to buy is a telltale sign to them that something is not normal. It sets off an alarm in their heads that this must be 'one-of-those-things'. Not a good thing.

Picture this: The cable TV guy has just finished installing your cable TV hookup. You've just signed the order and made your payment. Before he goes he says:

> "You know, Mrs. Jones, we make good
> money doing this. And we're looking for
> people to help us sell cable TV. It's really

easy; anyone can do it. All you have to do is share it with your friends and family. You know, like recommending a movie. And we're the best cable company in the country. How about it? You want to make some extra money with us?"

What's your gut reaction? Here's what my students have said:

"I'd laugh."

"I wonder if I overpaid…"

"I'd be surprised. Why ask me? I don't know anything about that."

"I'd wonder if they're financially in some kind of trouble."

"What kind of cable-TV company is this?"

"I don't want to sell cable TV."

Pretend that the next week, the phone rings and it's the cable-TV man. He says:

"Hi Mrs. Jones…this is the cable-TV man. Say we're still looking for people…

You know, it could be your ticket to financial freedom. Do you want to talk to my supervisor who has made a lot of money doing this? He just bought a vacation home in Hawaii. How about it? You want to make some money with us? It's really easy. Everyone wants cable..."

The next week, he calls again. Same pitch. And the next week again.

How are you feeling right now about your cable-TV service? By now the entire class says they'd dump the service and find another cable TV company.

How often has this happened to you with your customers? Have you lost some when you tried to get them into the business?

When someone hears their name and they want to try the product like a normal consumer, can you let them just be a regular, loyal customer? Without foisting the business on them?

But, says the die-hard recruiter, doesn't everyone want financial freedom? Or at least get their products or services at a discount for referring others to them?

NO. NO. NO.

Look around your house, your office, or your garage. Do you see things you really love? Your Mac? That Range Rover? The Cuisinart or espresso maker or your digital big-screen TV? So does that mean you want to sell those things for a living? Even if you're desperate for money? Most consumers don't either.

This is a BIG reason huge numbers of people don't buy from people in the direct sales or network marketing business -- because they do NOT want to be hounded to sell the stuff they just bought. They just want the product or service, like any other product or service they get.

Think about it. Would you use your cable TV service if they chased you to sell it? What about your AOL? Would you have gotten it if they had insisted you sell it too?

Ask yourself: **Would you use your product if you weren't selling it? Do you think others might too? Can you let customers be customers?**

Let me tell you what happened to me years ago. It still hurts when I think about it.

Stella's Story

I got one of my very best recruits about a year into my fifth business. She was a wonderful European lady who was co-owner of a fast food restaurant chain with her husband. She was a "born entrepreneur" and she, I, and the business hit it off with a bang.

About five months into the business, she had done so well, that her check for the month from the company was nearly $10k.

One day, she told me about an outing she was attending on a friend's yacht. She bought a lot of product to take with her, since she figured some of the attendees would want to buy some and the party hostess had asked her to do a show-and-tell. She was delighted about the prospect and I was too.

166

For three days after the event, she didn't call.

Day four, she called. "Kim, I have to tell you something you aren't going to like. I don't like it either. I am quitting the business. Let me tell you why I must do this. The hostess of the yachting party is a major friend of ours, and a big contributor to our church and the causes we all work for. And several of the guests came to her afterwards and asked that she not allow anyone to sell anything at these outings again. They didn't want anyone to take advantage of these contacts to sell them things. It was too hard to say 'no' for some, and others didn't like it, period. So she asked me not to come anymore unless I agreed not to offer anything for sale to the others anymore."

While I stood there speechless and in shock, Stella told me that although she loved the business and loved the income, she wouldn't do it anymore. Her friends and social life were too important to her. She did not want to lose her social life.

And of course, I understood, right? Of course.

I was stunned. Distraught. She was scheduled to be the keynote speaker at our next week's event with nearly 500 people coming, in large part to hear HER story. What would I tell them all? Oy vey.

I covered at the event, of course, since I was putting it on.

But I learned a painful lesson: For some really good entrepreneurs, it's not the money; it's not the vision; it's not the dream. She HAD all that. She did NOT want to trade in her social life and her social activities for the business. Period. I had to respect it. And I have learned to accept it because it is not under my control.

Many people don't need or want the added income enough to put their social relationships and their emotions at risk. Yes, some of them may still vent about not having enough income. But they'd rather do that, and have less of it, or perhaps do a different kind of business, than this one where their friends are the main market.

Can you accept that and let go? When you get a new customer, let THEM ask you about the business, not the other way around. You've dropped the hint. Remember you said, "I liked the product so much I decided to go into business…" Now let go. Deal?

The Good News about Customers

The good news about lots of happy customers is this: Among them are the few who love it so much they'll ask you how to make it available to others. What if that happens every now and then? ☺ Most companies with established product lines say that for every hundred regular customers they have, two or three also sell the product. That's 2 or 3 percent. Remember also that many top distributors started as happy customers.

That's how I started my first network marketing business. I liked the water filter a professor was selling in the back of a tai chi class so much that I asked him how I could start selling it too.

One lady reported in class that an old acquaintance she called with her new First Date Script liked the new approach so much that she signed up with her on the spot as a distributor! The acquaintance said she had been a networker before, was looking to get back into it, and wanted to be able to approach people with the same script she had just heard herself.

Ray's Confession

Ray Gebauer, a network marketer of many years who achieved the top level in his company, is now telling his people the same thing. Here is a letter he emailed to his group of thousands of network marketers on September 30, 2003. He entitled the email "Confession – I was wrong". Here are excerpts from that letter.

"Dear Mannatech family and team,

"I confess -- I was wrong...

"I've believed for years that the smartest and fastest way to help the most people in Mannatech reach the most people, and make the most money, was by looking primarily for and targeting the entrepreneur, or what we often refer to as a business builder.

"I believed that it was almost a waste of time to find customers.

"Here is why I now believe I was wrong.

"The undeniable fact is that 100% of my volume, and yours too, is from consumers (all business builders are consumers too). Of that 100% volume, probably less than 1% is from people who order strictly because they are in this for the business and the money potential...

"I have promoted the idea that everyone should be focused primarily on recruiting people into the business.

"So, what is wrong with that?

"By telling everyone that they need to sell the business to everyone, I've basically disempowered almost everyone, because very few are comfortable or effective at selling [the business].

"What people are comfortable with is talking about the products and what the products have done for them.

"But even THAT ends up being ineffective for most associates, because what has been modeled for them is "seller talk," which turns off 95% of the prospects. Instead of attracting them, we inadvertently repel them, blaming them for not caring about their health, or being closed-minded or even stupid…

"That is why I so appreciate the gift that Kim Klaver is offering us in her incredible Three Scripts Class that shows us how to get rid of the conditioning and mindset of sales and science that is hurting us far more than helping us. Her non-sales approach is easy and fun to use and attracts people, instead of accidentally repelling them.

"I now see how using this approach, you could reach Presidential [$60,000 volume] in 6 to 9 months without ever recruiting a single business builder…"

If more and more of us give customers their rightful place in our business, network marketing may soon become the business of choice for serious entrepreneurs.

<u>*Fourth Agreeement:*</u>

Do it over and over and over and over and over and over and over

> *"There have now been many studies of elite performers — international violinists, chess grand masters, professional ice-skaters, and so forth — and the biggest difference researchers find between them and lesser performers is the cumulative amount of deliberate practice they've had. Indeed, **the most important talent may be the talent for practice itself...** "*
>
> Atul Gawande
> *Complications 2002, p. 20*

*D*o you want it in your lifetime? I mean, the regular income that 100, 300, 1000 regular customers could bring? ...

I won't promise that it will happen for you, but what if it happens for you the way it did for me? ...

What did I do to make it happen? Let me tell you, now that I know what I did then. I put myself in

my consumer's shoes and said words that opened their
minds, or that led them to tell me quickly that they
weren't the one I was calling.   I protected my self-
esteem by letting the wrong ones go and saying *No* first
as often as I could.   Then I put out my favorite hot
button over and over and over and over and over and
over and over.   Until I could do it in my sleep, day or
night, drunk or sober, when I was exhausted, depressed
or upset.

     The new scripts and the concepts underlying
them are not what people expect. Sellers don't expect to
speak to prospects this way, nor do prospects expect
sellers to present their wares this way. And scripts are
the opposite of what sales people usually learn to say.

     People who use them report that the words open
the minds of consumers. When they hear the First Date
Script or Scripts 1, 2 or 3, consumers suddenly perceive
the seller as an advisor and friend, rather than a dreaded
seller who will pressure them into buying.

     There was a time when I, too, used some seller
talk. Years ago, I discovered the words that opened

consumers' minds and I worked hard at using them consistently. Now the words come out of my mouth by themselves. They're part of me for any hot button I choose.

They could be part of you too -- if you practice like I did.

Here's what to do as soon as you put this book down.

1.   Have your final First Date Script, and your Scripts 1, 2 and 3 on cards or in your PDA, so that you can carry them with you everywhere.

2.   Practice your scripts OUT LOUD at least 7 times a day, 21 days in a row. In front of the mirror, to the dog, or to an accommodating spouse or roommate. Memorize them.

If you miss a day, start over. This helps fine tune your script, and make it second nature in case someone asks you what you do when you're not expecting it. Or in case someone says, "That sounds like me too. How much is it?" ...

If you don't practice starting the moment you put this book down, your brain will start forgetting the fine points it just learned. Because doing them is not natural for you – yet.

3.   **Treat key phrases as if they were one long word**. For example, think of the End Question ("Do you know anyone who might like to know about a product like that?") as one long word, kind of like "antidisestablishmentarianism" if you hail from the 60's, or the catchy Mary Poppins' "supercalifragilistic-expialidocious". It is, perhaps, the most important phrase you'll use, tied for first place with your Opener and Market Segment.

Let me tell you what happened to a Three Scripts class graduate who didn't realize the importance of the exact wording of the End Question. At Study Hall she reported that she had called 17 relatives and friends and got no orders or referrals. Not even one. I asked her what she had said to them. She recited her script and ended with "Who do you know like that?" The gasps from the people in the Study Hall mirrored the pressure

177

that this graduate's relatives and friends must have felt too.

Other deviations from The End Question that graduates have found themselves saying is: "Are you interested in a product like that?" or "Who do you know who's interested in a product like that?" These are too pressure-filled for most people and one can feel them backing away as these words come out.

Most intelligent human beings learn by remembering the gist of some information they hear from a teacher, and then saying it in their own words. This is the reverse. YOU provide the specific information from your Remembering Room and say it in the Three Scripts words! At least the key phrases.

These scripting formulas seem to work in a wide variety of selling situations.

Julia L of Shaklee, for example, used the First Date Scripting formula to introduce the Three Scripts class to one of her people who almost never took her suggestions. Here's what Julia said to her doubting downline:

"I just took a class for distributors who don't know what to say to introduce people to their products, or who know they're saying the wrong thing, like what used to happen to me. I never used to know what to say about our product that helped me get rid of my hot flashes. I'd stumble over my words and say something vague. Then I'd feel the people turning off. At this class Kim helped me create a script and now I don't stumble over my words anymore. Last night I used my new script at a bridge game and the two women there ordered the product. I wasn't even shy about saying it in front of their husbands. Do you know anyone who might like to take a class like that?"

Her downline took the class.

John Fogg, founder of The Greatest Networkers.com website and a well known author in our industry, used the End Question to promote the e-book version of this book in a recent email to his members.

He began that email by saying, "The self-proclaimed President of I Really HATE Scripts International (that's me) has changed his mind!" After describing some e-book highlights, he wrote:

"Do you know anyone who might like to know about a book like that?"

Then, in his elegant professorial fashion, he pointed out that the End Question "takes all the pressure off. Now it's not a sales 'close,' it's an opening for referrals...".[37]

Cold Cadaver Calling™

Practicing on the dog helps get the words down, but for many people it is not enough. It doesn't get rid of the heebies -- the knots in the stomach that prevent one from picking up the phone to make a sales call with a real person at the other end of the line.

Calling cold cadavers has solved that problem for many who have attended the Three Scripts Study Halls.

---

[37] Email from John Fogg to Kim Klaver, 2/4/04. See http://whowho911.com/new_book.html

Just like working on cadavers relieves medical students of the fear of puncturing a lung or cutting off the wrong organ.

Our cadavers have been either opportunity seeker leads from a leads company or listings in the local white pages of the phone book. The likelihood of these leads turning into a customer is so low that it doesn't matter if you blow it. The value they have is to give you practice talking to real people. The mirror, the dog, and the spouse go only so far..

The idea is to connect with a minimum of 100 people per week, so that you can practice your script 100 times per week, minimum, for 4 weeks running.

Either leaving a message or talking to a live person counts. Hanging up after saying nothing, or wrong numbers do not.

No one expects to make a sale or get referrals, although once in a while someone gets them. The purpose is to FLEX YOUR SPEAKING MUSCLES. Like weight trainers pump iron, you pump your speaking skills with cold cadaver calls.

Three tips for Cold Cadaver Calling:

1. You can use either your full First Date Script or just the Short First Date Script as your opener. Here's an example of the Short First Date Script.

Opener (same for all examples): "Hello, I'm looking for Mary Jones. Is she there? …

OK. Great. This is Lulu Sweet and I'm a local merchant (or business owner) in town. I'm calling everyone in my neighborhood to ask them a question. Do you have a minute?…

Example A. "My company is introducing a product for people who are extremely overweight like I was, and have never had success in keeping it off and who don't want to staple their stomachs. Do you know anyone around here who might like to know about a product like that?"

Example B. "My company is introducing a product for parents with kids who are picky eaters, like me, and they want to make sure the kids get proper nutrition. Do you think anyone around here might like to know about a product like that?"

Example C. "I'm introducing a service for men who hate shopping, like I do. Do you know anyone who might like to know about a service like that?"

After you've done 100 calls using your Short First Date Script, do another 100 with the First Date Script, or vice versa, your choice. Do that each week until the whole script rolls off your tongue and you sound just as friendly as you would talking to an old friend at your kitchen table.

2.   Notice that instead of saying "I market a product…", you now say "My company is introducing a product.." This opener is more effective when you initiate a marketing conversation.

3.   Find a buddy to do the calls with, even if you think you can do them by yourself. A buddy will hear bits of seller talk that might have crept into your

script by mistake. Like "Oh it's wonderful" or "I'm so excited," etc.

Buddies and Study Halls: Companionship and Accountability vs. Confidence and Belief

A buddy is a substitute for self-confidence. Many people will do things with a buddy that they don't do by themselves, like exercising early in the morning or making sales calls. You giggle together, you blow calls together, you get scared together. You lend each other your mental attitude, so that you do the calling instead of the filing.

Study Hall was designed to help graduates of the Three Scripts classes do the practice necessary to get their customer business off the ground. It's turning out to be the high point of the week for many participants who are eager to report what they did. Even if they didn't do as much as they committed to, they enjoy reporting that they did something. Plus, new scripts are cooked up, problems are brought up and solved, and others tell what they're doing that's working, from hosting home parties to building their own catalog empires.

It doesn't matter if you have no confidence. Get a buddy and bumble together. Pretty soon you'll both be making those calls with new confidence. And it doesn't matter if you're too new to have belief in your business, or if all the failure and rejection you've suffered have eroded your vision. People do those calls so that they can have something exciting to report at the next Study Hall. They report that just doing the calls each week has increased their confidence.

And we can't wait to hear your stories.

After all that practice, what if now you're ready to make a real call? Or go to a mixer? Or try it out on your weekly leads group? Perhaps you'll start thinking of old customers who haven't ordered for a while, or even friends or family whose numbers you put away a long time ago...

What if, with your new consumer scripts, people don't give you the "cold ear" anymore, or walk the other way when they see you coming?

Here's what happened to three ladies who took the Three Scripts class, and who have been participating in the Shaklee Study Halls for the last six weeks. These are excerpts from emails to me, or what they said during Study Hall. You can hear them, and more, online at http://whowho911.com/3scripts_studyhall.html

Miriam G, 10-year vet:

"For years before I took the 3-Scripts course I always avoided going to any mixers, for fear someone would ask me what I did. Let me tell you what has happened. Since the course, I am so prepared to answer the dreaded question [What do you do?], that when I went to a Chamber mixer last night I was what my sons would call a 'babe magnet'. I never have felt so attractive in my life. It felt GREAT.

"I was so ready with a script for what I did, that the confidence and passion for what I do acted like a magnet. People wanted to know what I did, and asked. My answer: 'I market a product for people who have aches and pains, and don't want to do drugs, like me. Before I tried this system, I was feeling like I was pushing 70 instead of 50. Within about two weeks of going on the product, I started feeling like I did when I was 25. Do you know anyone who would like to know about a product like that?'

"I had a steady stream of attracted people, coming up to me the whole evening. Talk about having fun getting great leads... Thank you Kim for a class that has truly altered the course of my business. I've been doing it 10 years and now it's a whole new day."

Mary A, 31-year vet:

"This Three Scripts class has totally changed my business and my life. Here's my history of volume since doing Three Scripts: Month 1 - up $500, Month 2 - up $1000, Month 3 - up $1500.

"I never made calls before because I didn't know what to say. Now I LOVE doing it. I used to be so afraid to call, but now they're all saying 'thank you so much for calling!' I'm so amazed!"

Janet O, 17-year vet

"I am speechless, I can't believe what's going on since taking the course and doing Study Hall. I've done double the volume. $1500 PV last week, another $2100 this week, all based on the 86 calls I did last week – plus I did 10 this week…

"For the first time, I am enjoying this – I am having a response back. The scripts give me what to say, and Study Hall makes me do

it. The fun is back in Shaklee. I came to the
course hoping to find my spark again, but I
found a fire instead. I thought I might quit,
but now I'm on fire..."

I wish I had room to print all the other messages
I've been receiving from people who report similar
increases in business volume, driven by the fire that their
new scripts have lighted inside.[38]

Few of the successes came instantly, however.
The three ladies above practiced their scripts until they
were confident enough to use them in public. And
everyone in the Study Halls is doing the same. They're
practicing first in front of the mirror or with their dog.
Then they get a buddy and try it, often on cadavers
first...

How long will it take to get good?

Tony Robbins once posed this question: "If it
takes 84 times to practice something before you get good

---

[38] Some are posted on my web site http://whowho911.com/

at it, how long will that take?"

Say it takes practicing your First Date Script 84 times to get good at it:

QUIZ

1. If you practiced it once a year, how long will it take to get pretty good at it?
2. What if you practiced it once a month?
3. How about once a week?
4. Once a day?
5. Seven times a day?
6. Twelve times a day?

ANSWER: From 84 years to seven days.

Moral: The more often you practice and the closer together the practices are, the better you get in less time.

Tony says that if you want "unconscious competence" where you do it without thinking, you need to practice 7 times a day, for 21 days in a row.

People are surprised when I tell them that the successes I have enjoyed have not come easily. I, too, had to do my thing over and over and over and over and over and over and over. I do not claim any innate talents, nor was I a born marketer. And I have never been a fast learner.

As a kid, I learned to play piano slowly and painfully, doing hours of Hannon scales under the impatient eye of my mother, a concert pianist. To my surprise, I got better, and I liked that feeling so much, I can still remember secretly enjoying practicing. And one day, I could play Beethoven's Moonlight Sonata by heart. Not as well as Van Cliburn, but well enough so that even I enjoyed listening to myself.

Learning to use computers was another challenge. I hated that I couldn't understand the software manuals that came with the computer programs I had just bought. I had to swallow my pride and buy the kindergarten software book series from companies like Peachpit Press, who specialize in helping people like me.

Even tennis, which I seem to have a knack for, was something I had to practice hours everyday if I wanted to win in the state matches.

What has helped me stick to difficult endeavors over the years are the stories about people who succeeded big time in fields they knew nothing about when they started, or for which they had no special knack. They just had a big desire for it. They had a reason to care about it and to practice doing it over and over and over and over and over and over and over until they could do it better.

Seeing some improvement, no matter how small, encourages me to keep on. Each improvement is proof that I can get better at something. Given enough time, I could become expert in anything I choose.

The surgeon Atul Gawande, in his inspiring book *Complications*, summarizes his own 11-year journey to becoming a recognized surgeon:

> "I am, I have found, neither gifted nor maladroit. With practice and more practice, I get the hang of it." (p. 22)

He adds that in medicine "we want perfection without practice," but this is not possible, either in medicine or in life.

Practice means you make mistakes. Everyone hates that. But you practice more and more until you get it right – at least more often than you did before.

Ben Hogan , the golf great, once told an aspiring golfer:

"Everyday you don't practice you're one day further from being good."[39]

Did you know that both Michael Jordan, NBA superstar, and Jerry Rice, NFL receiver of the year for most of his career with the San Francisco 49ers, practiced more than any of their teammates? And Mozart, the child prodigy, practiced so much that his hands were deformed by the time he was 28.

Without surrendering to constant practice like these greats, getting good at anything couldn't have happened for me.

---

[39] In Twyla Tharp, p. 32

Shall we do the Fourth Agreement now? I'll be doing it with you...

Fourth Agreement

Do it over and over and over and over and over and over and over

Close your eyes and say it out loud, with all your heart.

Part Two

100 Customers in 100 Days

The Launch

Time to put the pedal to the metal with real prospects, some of whom might actually be those one-in-tens we're all dreaming about. Long term, regular customers.

But where are we going to get them?

Who are we going to say our beautiful scripts to — other than the dog, the parakeet or cold cadavers?

Surprise! The easiest place to start is turning out to be **warm market** — anyone who knows your name. Family, friends, old high school classmates. old customers, dead downline.

I know that these people have been the most painful source of pukeyness, but let me tell you what's been happening to Three Scripts graduates. They've called a friend or relative thinking for sure that the person would say "Don't call me with this anymore."

Just like they've said in the past. Instead, however, my graduates are reporting that when they say the last line of the script – "Do you know anyone who might like to know about a product like that?" they can hear the sigh of relief over the phone. More often than ever before, they'll get at least a referral, if not an order. Best of all, they're having pleasant conversations. And they still have a place to go for Christmas dinner.

Here are comments from a couple of graduates who used their new scripts on their warm market. (More in the 'Warm Market' chapter coming up.)

Ruth Ann of Mannatech spoke to 50 in her warm market and got 9 orders, for a total of about $900 in volume. She said:

> " I could tell there was some reserve during the script. But when I said the last line ['Do you know anyone who might like to know about a product like that?'], I could feel them relaxing over the phone..."

Sandra of Isagenix talked with 13 people she knew and got 2 long-term autoship customers and 3 referrals, one of whom is a health club owner. She said:

"Nothing like this has ever happened to me before. It's fun to work now."

The **cold market** is a fine source of regular customers too – especially if you have had previous experience with the cold market and if you have the stamina and budget to handle it. Short First Date Scripts break the ice quickly with local entrepreneurs, cold leads, and bump-into's; and full First Date Scripts pared down to 30-seconds make effective commercials for leads groups.[40] A number of graduates have won 'commercial-of the-week' prizes in their leads groups.

Here's a cold market story from Rhonda B of Neways, Australia, whose husband went door to door with new downline in tow. (More stories in the cold market chapter coming up.)

---

[40] Full First Date Scripts are AT MOST 45 seconds long. Most leads groups limit informercials to 30 seconds.

"After I told my husband about the order I got with my new first date script from the bank teller, he decided to make up his own script and off he went doorknocking (house to house) with one of our new 'babies.' They knocked on 54 doors; 24 were home. Out of the 24, 8 said "No", 3 bought the starter pack on the spot and the rest are interested, to be followed up.

"My husband and his new downline went out the next day and did one street only and sold one starter pack and signed a lady up who had watched them walk the whole street and was waiting her turn. She said she had been prospected before and was waiting for someone like us to come and sign her up.

"We have been with Neways six years. We've never come across anything like what you're teaching and have always struggled between whether we should just do business or product…. Now we feel hope where there was lots of frustration before."

You can also use your scripts and the scripting concepts on the **Internet.** Email bylines based on your favorite fix can turn any email message into a viral marketing tool, and end up on business cards and brochure labels. If you are serious about using the internet for marketing, you can create a customer acquisition page through the Alternative Network Marketing (ANM) web site and run customer leads through it.

Here's what a Three Scripts grad who has been using an ANM customer site told people on a conference call with me about the customer sites.

"… I've had my site with Kim for two months. I'm new at this too and I've learned a lot. I've already put in 6 new customers with this site. And they were national. I never would have gotten them from my warm market. I got them just

from sending them to my customer site.
And I just started sending them 3 weeks
ago… I think Kim's site is the best thing
that's ever happened in the business."

– Deb B, Ideal Health

You can hear this story in Deb's own voice online at
http://www.alternativenetworkmarketing.com/

Parts of your scripts may also find their way into
messages you leave on prospects' voice mail and into the
ones you record on your answering machine. Graduates
report an unprecedented number of callbacks, and even
some sales, from the new messages they've been leaving
for people they've called. Here's what happened for Kay
E of Shaklee:

"… I reviewed the script and started
making the calls. I started with this guy I
talked to before on a cold call, who had said
he wasn't interested in our basic package…
No answer, so I left a message the way you
taught us to do it.

"Then I did another cold call... Right after that, the phone rings, and it's the first guy -- he called me back! And that has NEVER happened before with these cold calls. That's what got me just so fired up. So I did the script and ended with the "Do you know anyone" question. He said "Me!"

"Well, he ordered the basic package – and I did the thing about "cheaper by the dozen" and he became a member! So he's a regular monthly customer...

I actually put what you taught me into practice, and the results validated for me that it works..."

Finally, the chapter on **'Referrals'** gives you the words to say to referrals, which grads have reported they're receiving in unprecedented numbers. Sandra M. reports:

"I've been doing the Shaklee business for 10 years. And I've been stuck at the minimum for so long - I'm just sick and tired of it.   I've been to seminars, I've been to meetings, I've read books, I've learned scripts before - but they weren't me and they just didn't work for me.

So then I decided to take Kim Klaver's 3 Scripts class and I just finished it last week.

I've noticed a huge difference in my business already.

I knew my old way of talking to people was ALL wrong, and I had this appointment the day after I graduated from the class. So I'm practicing my script in the car on the way to see this lady, and even though **I started with my old seller talk, I saw the old glazed look coming into her eyes, and I QUICK fixed it and did my new script instead...**

She LIT UP, and said that sounded like her husband. She gave me three

referrals - one was herself, plus two others.

In 10 years of doing the business, I have never gotten a referral from a stranger... It already feels like I'm getting unstuck in the business and it's only been 7 days. You have to say something to the people, and I've learned now that you might as well say the right thing. Now I do!"[41]

Part Two is the big marketing pot from which you can choose what you want to do to get those 100, 300 or 1000 customers, who will give you your MCII – **M**onthly **C**ustomer **I**nsurance **In**come. The next chapters lay out how to use the three scripts in a variety of situations -- with your friends and family, old customers, catalog customers, local business owners, cold leads, and bump-into's. It gives you two straightforward techniques to get customers on the

---

[41] This is on audio also at http://www.WhoWho911.com/shaklee-class.html

internet, and shows you how to use your scripts to leave messages and record your own answering machine message.

You choose what you want to do, and the order and the intensity with which you do them. You can choose to be on the fast track, the medium track, or the leisure track. The approaches and techniques are the same. Like ordering a large, medium or small cup of coffee from the same fresh pot. You decide how much.

Before You Begin...

Regardless of what you decide to do or how much time or money you have to spend on getting your 100+ customers, you must be prepared to reach out effectively and efficiently. If you want it in your lifetime, that is ...

Here's a Checklist.

1.   Do you have a First Date Script (FDS) that you love madly?

The First Date Scripts you've read in the chapters above may seem easy to duplicate. They're not. They were the result of doing each step as they are described in Chapters 5-8. Fill in each box according to instructions. Read the instructions slowly. Little things make the difference between words that catch the attention of a consumer who's ready to buy and words that a consumer is likely to dismiss as just so much more seller talk. The Remembering Room step is a must. Follow the First Date Scripting Formula on page 127, and review the "Tips to Make Your Script Zing" right after that.

I cannot emphasize this enough. Students who spent as much time as necessary to follow the instructions in Chapters 5-8 produced scripts that were perfect or nearly perfect. They were consumer talk, not seller talk. Students who rushed through it, or skipped the Remembering Room altogether, produced scripts that had seller talk or were too vague or too long to be effective. People didn't respond. And so they had to start over.

If, after you've done everything outlined in the book, you want to make sure you have a good First Date Script, you may want to participate in a Script Clinic. (See 'Three Scripts Resources' at the end of the book.)

2. **Do you know the movable and interchangeable parts of your scripts,** such as the Opener and the End Question, your Market Segment, and your Personal Zingers? Each part is illustrated and its function explained in Chapter 8.

3. **Have you put your FDS (First Date Script), and all the pieces of Scripts 1, 2 and 3 that you will use, on sheets of paper, or cards, or in your PDA?** Keep them by your phone and in your pocket or purse so you have them available wherever you are.

4. **Have you practiced your scripts** 7 times a day, 21 days in a row? In front of the mirror, on your dog, cat, fish, parakeet or other admiring pet? Then, on cadavers, as described in Chapter 11, so you're ready to use it any time anywhere?

5. **Have you memorized all your scripts** so that you can say them in your sleep, day or night,

drunk or sober, when you're exhausted, depressed or upset? And still sound friendly and natural?

Memorizing your scripts will help you overcome the urge to change the words or the phrasing. Seller talk habits are often an unconscious part of your old selling conversations, and seller talk may creep in if you haven't made your new scripts a habit.

OK. That's it for preparing. Ready to launch?

Finding Your Audience

To the market we go.

It's a very big marketplace out there. In the U.S. alone, some 300 million people are milling about.

You have probably figured out by now from your own experience that everyone will not want to buy what you have. No matter how much you want it for them. (You don't buy everything that you hear is great either, do you?) For nine in ten people, your thing may not be on their radar at all, or it's still on their Vent List. So instead, you seek those one-in-ten who are looking for the fix that YOU feel strongly about. Their hot button is the same as yours!

These people are your audience.

In the movie business, people talk about a movie having to "find its audience" – those people who are likely to be attracted to that specific movie or type of movie. Consider a Frankenstein flick. Or *Schindler's List*. Or *Lord of the Rings*. Would you be attracted to all three? While a few people might, most people would be most strongly attracted to one.

How do movies 'find' their audience?

Apparently NOT by playing to them. When a writer or director tries hard to play to a general audience, the story ends up being weak, and despite lots of expensive special effects and massive marketing, audiences do not respond and the movie bombs at the box office.

Like one of Disney's recent films, *Alamo*. They spent around $125 million making it, and they're expecting less than $10 million back, based on domestic ticket sales. Some of the biggest budget movies were flops -- *Cutthroat Island* lost $81 million, *Ishta*r $47 mil, and *Santa Claus* $37 mil, to name just a few. [42]

---

[42] This and the other movie statistics in this paragraph are from the website at
http://66.102.7.104/search?q=cache:fMJFUVitZSIJ:news.bbc.co.uk/2/hi/e ntertainment/3621859.stm+why+movies+fail&hl=en&ie=UTF-8.

"The average movie now costs $64 million to make and another $39 million to market, according to the Motion Picture Association of America. And, "in the last five years maybe 6 pictures out of 1,000 recouped their cost in the theatrical marketplace," said Nick Coulter, president of Studio Alliance. "Today the hits have to make up for the losses."[43] It's like gambling. But they keep doing it in the hopes that someday they'll win big – like *Titanic* or *ET*.

The few movies that make it (i.e., take in more than they spent) are the ones that find their audience. They don't play to an audience or try to find the collective audience's hot button. They focus on telling a story they really, really want to tell, even if it goes against prevailing opinion. They create a following, despite rejection by the big studios.

Mel Gibson financed and distributed his own movie because no one would do it – none of the big guys, that is. He wasn't 'playing to the audiences' they

---

[43] New York Times, p. B8, 4/20/04

knew. He was doing his movie because HE liked it. He was telling HIS story, not wondering what story would sell. He was leading with HIS hot button. And those who shared it came. And because it was controversial and made the news big time, others came to see what the hoopla was all about.

As of May 2004, the *Passion of the Christ* has taken in $364 million in the US, and it is now the #1 grossing independently produced movie in history. He led with his own hot button, and paid no attention to anyone else's.

Guess who's second? Yep. *My Big Fat Greek Wedding*. Another movie no one wanted to finance because they didn't think it had 'a big enough audience.' The writer Nia Vardallos did a stand-up comedy routine in an L.A. nightclub, about a Greek girl marrying an American boy, until Tom Hanks came along and offered to underwrite her act and make it into a movie. She was so ready for that break, she already had her own screenplay written! She didn't care about the audience out there, or how to impress them. She wanted to tell

215

HER story. She said that she'd have been happy if her movie had only played on video in the basements of Greek churches.

Greek Wedding has taken in over $300 million. Nia Vardallos went with HER hot button and paid no attention to anyone else's. Those who shared hers, came.

Sofia Coppola won an Oscar for Best Screenplay in 2004 for her movie *Lost in Translation*. When she was notified that she had been nominated, here's what she said:

> "It's really hard to digest. When you're thinking about something personal, when you're not thinking about the audience, it's exciting when people connect to what you're thinking about. There's nothing better than that."[44]

She led with her hot button. Developed a screenplay about it, and went to market with it. She

---

[44] *New York Times*, 1/28/04.

wasn't thinking about pleasing some audience; she was telling HER story.

Who really knows how to impress an audience for sure, anyway? Who knows what really is on a person's Change List? Who knows what a stranger's hot button is?

That 'something personal' Ms. Coppola referred to, is, for each one of us, that big hot button, that Favorite Fix, the personal zingers, the life-altering results we each get from our thing.

The stronger your feelings are about it, the more effective you'll be in drawing the audience who are ready for your fix. People who are health conscious and can't stand their hot flashes will be attracted to someone who says with authenticity that they no longer have them, and did it without drugs. People who have demanding jobs and no longer have the energy to do anything after work might be attracted to a hardworking daycare center owner who used to fall asleep babysitting her grandchildren, and now stays awake easily until the children fall asleep.

Like movie people, you go into the marketplace and find your audience – those people who are interested in your story. Then, some of them become like a fan club of the product, and you're the club director. They buy month after month after month. You might have a No More Achy Joints Club, someone else might have an I Don't Fall Asleep in the Afternoons Anymore Club. You specialize in a specific fix for people with certain needs, like a cardiac surgeon who focuses on people who have heart problems.

After you get your first 'hot button club' going strong with 100+ regular paying customers, you might start a second hot button club for another fix that you're excited about. Or you might stay with just one club, and become perceived as a specialist in that one fix. Your hot button club becomes the place to go for people who want it. You've found your audience. And they can find you, like they find the cardiologist.

Deadly Distractions

Perhaps the biggest obstacle to getting your 100 regular customers is the temptation to say Yes to opportunities to get involved in other 'clubs' -- other audiences, other fixes, other hot buttons.

For example, you've just started a No More Achy Joints Club, and a friend, who's also rep in your company, asks you to share a booth at a diabetes convention. You'll "save a lot of money because you can get the booth cheap," says your friend. And your company has products that have helped people with diabetes.

Trouble is, you have no personal experience with overcoming diabetes, either for yourself or someone close to you. You have no passion for it. It's just a selling opportunity.

Is that your audience? ...

So, **just say _No_**.

If you don't, it will become a deadly distraction – something that takes your focus away from YOUR hot button. It saps your energy, your time and your budget. And in the end, you can't help giving off the scent of a seller... Because the only reason you're doing the diabetes convention (or thinking about presenting the air machine to dentists, or giving a talk to the fibromyalgia support group, or some other audience) is because you came across a selling opportunity for your company's products.

It's easy to fall into the 'grasping-for-an-audience' mode in the beginning, when you don't have many customers yet, or when you're going through a difficult month. Even a new product launch by your own company can be a distraction if you change your focus to it.

If you find yourself grasping and losing your focus, go back to your Remembering Room to rekindle your hot button and remember why you chose it. Then think of all the people who are waiting for you to call their name - all future members of your hot button club.

That's how Mothers Against Drunk Driving (MADD) got so big. One Mom calling out her hot button name until she had groups of Moms who had also lost a dear child to a drunk driver – in every state across the country.

If you are active in your business, deadly distractions of all kinds will come across your desk. Just say *No* -- if you want it in your lifetime. At least until you get those 100 regular customers.

Three Tips To Keep Them Listening

Here are three little techniques to keep your prospect on the phone a few seconds longer...then a few more seconds... then a few more...

They all show the consumer that you respect their time, their intelligence and their role as decision maker. As Seth Godin says, respectful marketing

"is not just good manners, it's profitable... When we treat people with respect, they're more likely to do what we want... The only way to make a long-term profit is by respecting people." (2004, p. 114.)

So how do you do that?

1. Tell Them It'll Be Quick

In the opening line or two, signal that the call will be quick. Here's how: Add this phrase to your script:

"I only have a minute, and I'm calling you because..."

This brings immediate relief to people who are busy. It also tells them you will not be spending hours talking about the latest episode in Aunt Lulu's marital saga or her children's escapades. In cold market conversations, it quickly sets you apart from other sellers who tend to talk nonstop, trying to force the person to stay on the phone as long as they can.

2.   Say Goodbye First

Surprise your prospect. What person in sales do you know who ever said goodbye first?... Prospects usually end up saying whatever they need to, to squirm out of the conversation and get away.

Instead, add either of these phrases, or something similar, to your script:

"Gotta run – another call..."

"I have to run, I have another call, but I wanted you to know about it..."

You'll see how and when to use the 'It'll-be-quick' and 'Goodbye-first' phrases in the various scripts coming up. When you use them, your prospects will realize right off that you don't push or take up a lot of their time. And suprisingly, that you may not even need them. For some reason, that makes them more likely to take your calls.

3. The Fuller-Brush-Man Pause

"The Fuller Brush Man knew what he was doing. In the old days, Fuller's door-to-door salesmen learned a basic rule: After you ring the bell, take a step or two backward. That way, the woman of the house won't feel intimidated opening the door for a stranger..." (Seth Godin, 2004, p.114)

In telephone marketing, someone trained like the Fuller Brush Man would pause very early in their opening pitch, so that the person called won't feel like they're being invaded. A pause before you move on with your main script will give your callee a chance to engage in the conversation and feel in control.

Have you ever noticed how many telemarketers, once they have you on the phone, talk fast and non-stop for a whole minute or two? That's like jamming a foot in the door and not letting go until you force the surprised and dismayed woman of the house to let you in; only you've done it over the phone. Can they be happy about that? Or receptive? ...

That may be the biggest reason over 65 million people have registered with the Do Not Call Registry. Strangers calling and talking at them non-stop when they're having dinner.

So, add a Fuller-Brush-Man (FBM) pause every 15 to 20 seconds in your spiel, so the person has a chance to breathe and process your words. You "step back" in your approach, on the phone.

Here's an example. Say you're calling people in your neighborhood to introduce a new product.

YOU

Hi Mary Belle! This is Lulu Paws, and I live in the neighborhood.[45] I'm calling everyone in our neighborhood to ask them a question. Do you have a minute?

[FBM Pause]

> **CALLEE**
> OK. What's the question?

YOU

My company's introducing[46] a product for someone who has had trouble keeping the weight off for years, and who wants to try something new that's not drugs, like I did. Do you know anyone who might like to know about a product like that?"

---

[45] Other phrasing options depending on the size of your area are: 1) If you live in a large metropolitan area like Atlanta or L.A., you might try: "I live in zip code 00000 and I'm calling everyone in our zip code to ask them a question…" 2) If you live in a tiny town and you're targeting an area larger than your town, e.g. Corte Madera in Marin County, California, you might say, "I live in Corte Madera and I'm calling everyone in the area to ask them a question…" The key is to identify yourself as a member of the community of the person you're calling.

[46] OR "My company has introduced…" in the case of products that have been around for a while.

[FBM Pause]

> **CALLEE**
> Hmmm. How much weight did you lose?

YOU

45 pounds in 3 months. For years I'd been losing the same 20 pounds, then gaining it all back and more. I've done all the diets and bought all kinds of exercise machines, but nothing worked for long. Then I came across this product and in three months I lost 45 pounds. It's been 3 years now, and they've never come back. Anyway, I liked the product so much I decided to go into business to make it available to other people like me. And that's why I'm calling.

[FBM Pause to Breathe]

> **CALLEE**
> Hmmm. What's the product?...

YOU

[Follow-Up Script #1, Chapter 9]

When you haven't asked a question, but have paused to breathe like in the example above, you're allowing your callee to say something if they want to. Listen extra carefully so you don't charge ahead just as they're starting to say something. If they ask a question, respond to it, then segue into your Personal Zingers if appropriate.

Whenever you ask a question, wait for the reply. Even if there's a long silence. (long = more than 3 seconds.) Do not charge ahead to fill the silence, as so many people do, and, unwittingly, blurt out seller talk, like "and it's so exciting..." Who knows, Mary Belle might be thinking about someone she knows who might like to know about your product. Would you want to interrupt such a wonderful thought?

Always end with the End Question: "Do you know anyone who might like to know about a product like that?" Then keep silent. Practice it. You may feel a strong urge to say something to persuade the callee to buy. Bite your tongue instead and wait for their answer...

If They're a "Do Not Call"

While you may not be big enough to receive the 64 million names on the Do Not Call List, the customer's wishes always come first.

If they say they signed up for the Do Not Call list, apologize and tell them you'll take their name off your list. Identifying yourself as a member of their community may help reduce their feeling of being invaded. So far, there have been no reports of any screaming callees. Always be polite and put yourself in their shoes. You might say:

"I'm sorry. I'll take you off my list immediately. Have a great day."

OK. We're ready to start working on your first 100. Shall we?

Warm Market

The pukeys have left the building. In their place are family and friends who are giving referrals and ordering product. Or at least asking for information instead of criticizing and heading for the door.

A Three Scripts grad, who had not had good experiences selling to family in the past, reports:

"In the eight years I've been in marketing, my Mom has never shown interest in any product I've ever sold. Sure, she'd say,'Oh that's nice honey,' but she never bought. Then I changed my approach like you taught us in class, and after my 30-second script, she said "Order me some of that." I was in shock…"

-- Spencer L, ForMor

Many more members of the ongoing Study Halls are going to their warm market and reporting much more pleasant experiences and shock at their good results.

Ruth Ann of Mannatech spoke to 50 in her warm market and got 9 orders, for a total of about $900 in volume. She commented:

> "I could tell there was some reserve during the script, but when I said the last line ['Do you know anyone who might like to know about a product like that?'], I could feel them relaxing over the phone..."

Jan H of Melaleuca talked to 43 friends and family members and got 3 new customers, 8 referrals and 6 people who said they'd give Jan's number to others. So, while she got the "cold ear" from some, she told the group:

> "The results make me feel great."

Sandra of Isagenix talked with 13 people and got 2 long term autoship customers and 3 referrals, one of whom is a health club owner. She said:

"Nothing like this has ever happened to me before. It's fun to work now."

And John P of Mannatech reports to date that after three months of calling friends and relatives, he and an associate have gotten 60 customers. He says:

"My whole attitude is different... I have never called these people. I've never known what to say to them. Now it's so easy to share this with people..."

Guess what new thing John, Sandra, Jan, Joan, Ruth Ann and Spencer have been saying to get these reactions?

Your First Date Script (FDS) is in response to someone who just asked you "What do you do?" So, your opener is: "I market a product for someone who..." **But, <u>when you go first</u> – when you're the one opening the conversation or sending the email or letter** -- your opener is:

> *My company's <u>introducing</u>[47] a product for someone[48] who*

<u>The rest of the script remains the same.</u>

Warm Ears

Here's the opener for people who are **happy to hear from you** – the Warm Ears. They've forgotten or don't really care that you tried to sell them something in the past. They ask you how you are. For example:

YOU
Hi Aunt Lulu. This is Kim.

> **WARM EAR**
> Oh hi Kim. What's new with you?
>
> or: What have you been up to?
>
> or: What have you been doing?
>
> or: What's new in your life?
>
> or: other how-are-you question.

---

[47] OR "My company has introduced…" in the case of products that have been around for a while.
[48] or "people" or "women" or etc.

YOU
[Mirror what they say:]

Let me tell you what's new in my life.

or: **Let me tell you what I've been doing.**

or: **Here's what I've been up to.**

or: **Well, let me tell you what's new with me.**

or a mirror of whatever they said.

I only have a minute and I'm calling

everyone I know to ask them a question.

Do you have a minute? [Pause]

[This alerts the other person that this is
not a social visit. You're not calling to talk about
their high blood pressure or their marital problems.]

> **WARM EAR**
> Sure.

YOU

**My company's introducing** **a product for people**[49]
who…

---

[49] or "someone", or "women", etc. Whenever you see "for people who",
know that you can use "someone" or "women" or "men", etc. – whichever
word is appropriate for your market segment

+ Your full First Date Script

or Personal Market Segment Script

Do you know anyone who might like to know about a product like that?

Cold Ears

Here's the opener for **the people who you think will remember you as a seller bear**. The ones who are tired of hearing about your business or your products, and fear that you're calling to sell them your latest discovery. The only difference with Cold Ears is that they usually don't ask how you are, so you skip the line "Let me tell you how I'm doing."

Really important is to remember that they may change how they feel about your call in less than a minute – when they find out that you're only asking them if they know anyone who might want to know about a product like yours. That you're not selling them anything or begging them to go into business with you.

Here's how the conversation might go:

YOU

Hi Uncle Harry. This is Kim

> **COLD EAR**
>
> [Silence]
>
> or: Yeah? [with rising intonation]

YOU

I only have a minute because I'm calling everyone I know to ask them a question.

Do you have a minute?

> **COLD EAR**
>
> Yeah?

YOU

<u>I'm calling because my company's introducing</u> a product for people who...

> **+ Your full First Date Script or**
>
> **Short First Date Script**

Do you know anyone who might like to know about a product like that?

For both Warm and Cold Ears, depending on how well the person knows you, you can insert friendly phrases like "Remember when...". For example,

"Remember when I couldn't get up in the mornings after I had Lisa (your first baby)… blah blah blah…"

When the person realizes that you're not "selling them" or hounding them about a business, like you might have in the past, and that you're asking about someone in particular and that it's not necessarily them, the pressure they expected is off and they suddenly relax. Hundreds of people have reported this and all were pleasantly surprised. And, of course, they kept on dialing.

If you're not calling their name or the name of someone they know, they usually feel they can just say, "I don't know anyone offhand like that, but I'll keep my ears open." Or if they do identify with your story or know someone who does, they'll ask you for more information. Or they'll place an order on the spot. Or they'll give you a referral or two. Even the Cold Ears have surprised some of my graduates with an order.

Want to try it? Dredge up your old lists of family and friends and mark the ones you can bear to call again. Do it for just an hour and see what happens. If there's not a match, just treat it as though you called a wrong number: Tell yourself, "Sorry, no one by that name lives there. So, dial again, OK?"

One of my graduates, Janet H. of Melaleuca, said she was too scared to call her warm market, so instead she emailed them or wrote them letters. Here's what happened to her:

> "I have a list of 303 relatives. I was still a bit scared to call them, so I sent emails and letters to all of them last week using my new script. So far, I have 3 customers and some really nice email responses. I've never gotten such quick responses…"

So, pick your weapon and dive in…

Old Customers and Catalog Empires

Old Customers

Old customers are a surprisingly good source of new long term customers. Many have responded well to calls from Three Scripts graduates who are using their First Date Scripts.

You can email, write or call them. Calling yields the fastest responses, but of course, that's also the most risky for your attitude if your confidence is low…

Again, the new words to learn specifically for reviving old customers lies in the opening line.

[Ring ring]

YOU

Hi Mrs. Jones? … This is Kim Klaver, *your old*[50] *Company X rep. Remember me?*

---

[50] or "best" or "good", whichever is true

[Pause]

> **CALLEE**
> Yes… I think so…

YOU
Mrs. Jones, I only have a minute, but I'm calling all my old[51] customers because the company is introducing a product for someone who…

> **+ Your full First Date Script**
>
> **OR Short first Date Script**

Do you know anyone who might like to know about a product like that?

It's important to say "<u>the company</u> is introducing…" rather than "I'm introducing" or "We're introducing" so that you can separate yourself from the company and position yourself as an Advisor. Using "I" or "we" positions you immediately as a seller. And everything you say then becomes suspect. ☹

The phrase "I'm calling all my old/best/good customers" signals that what you're going to say is

---

[51] or "best" or "good", whichever is true

important enough to say to ALL the members of a select group. And "I only have a minute" signals that it's going to be short.

As in the previous examples, you can choose to use either your entire First Date Script or just your Short First Date Script. It depends on how much time you have, how familiar you are with your customer, and how comfortable you are with your script. Up to you.

Here's the script Bobbie C of Shaklee used with an old customer:

"Hi Mary, this is Bobbie, your old Shaklee rep.

"I only have a minute, but I'm calling all my old customers because the company is introducing a product for people who have achy knees when they go up and down stairs, like I used to. Do you have a minute?

"You know, 8 months ago I fell down the steps and hurt my knee. And ever since I had to have therapy because it hurt so

bad. My doctor gave me some drugs, but they gave me stomach problems and I was worried about other side effects. So I tried this new cream and rubbed it on my knee. And within 5 minutes I noticed the pain was almost gone. I immediately stopped the drugs and one week later I stopped the therapy. It's been 5 months now and my knee feels fine. And I can exercise again like I did before I got hurt. Do you know anyone who might like to know about a product like that?"

Here's her story of what happened:
"Last week I called an old customer – one of my non-member customers. This person who was not that enthusiastic of a customer to begin with, I called her and gave her my new script for the pain product. Her husband happens to be an orthopedic doctor, and <u>she said her husband might like that and she ordered it for him.</u>

"Then I went off script a bit, and asked her "Would he like the technical information on it?" And she said "Oh no he doesn't want that. If it works he might, but he doesn't want that." And I thought, ohhh, Kim is SO right...it was such a pointed affirmation of what she has been telling us for weeks - not to lead with the science..."

> Bobbie C, Shaklee rep
> for 27 years.

Bobbie used her full First Date Script because she knew the customer quite well. If she barely knew the customer, she might have used the short Personal Market Segment version:

"Hi Mary, this is Bobbie, your old Shaklee rep. Remember me? ...

"I only have a minute, but I'm calling all my old customers because the company is introducing a product for people who have achy knees when they go up and

down stairs, like I used to. Do you know anyone who might like to know about a product like that?" ...

Then, if her customer showed some interest, she could slide in her personal zingers and results later in the conversation, as we showed in Chapter 9.

Catalog Empires

This strategy is for distributors in companies who put out a catalog several times a year.

As soon as you know that your customers should have received their catalogs, get your customer list together and make your calls. Make two lists: one for customers who are using your products, and one for old customers who have stopped using your products and may not remember you at all. The scripts are identical, except for the parts that are boldfaced. The parts in parentheses and underlined are those that vary with each new catalog and with different personal market segments.

Call to a Current Product User

Hello, Mona Lisa? [*Pause*]

Hi! This is Lulu, your Company X rep.

Do you have a short minute? [*Pause.*]

OK, good. I'm calling because the company has just sent out a catalog. It's the one with (the family by their pool) on the cover. Anyway, on page (6), they're running a special on a product for people who (know about Botox, but would like to try a natural alternative). **I thought of you since I know we talked about this kind of product before, and now they're running a special on it.** I have to run, I have another call, but I wanted you to know about it, OK? It's page (6). OK? Gotta run. Bye!

Of course, if they want to order, TAKE THE ORDER, even if you've said "I've got to run…" You can always say: " Sure, I can take your order now. It won't take long." Do NOT send them to the website, unless they ask specifically for the website. A spontaneous reaction from them requires the same from you.

Sometimes old customers say they'll check out their order page later, and they do just that. Many students have reported getting orders the customers placed themselves, for $100 to nearly $1,000 a day or two after these calls.

Call to an Old Customer Who May Not Remember You at All

Hello, I'm looking for Cleopatra Smith, is she there? [*Pause*]

Hi! This is Lulu, your **old** COMPANY X rep. **Remember me?** [*Pause*]

I only have a minute, and I'm calling because the company has just sent out a catalog, it's the one with (the woman with the plaid shirt on the cover). Anyway, on page (9), they're introducing a product for people who (have had little aches and pains in their joints that are getting worse, and

<u>they'd like to try something new that's not drugs)</u>. **I'm calling you in case you know anyone who might like to know about a product like that.** I have to run, I have another call, but I wanted you to know about it, OK? It's page (9). Gotta run, I have another call! Bye!

I am assuming that you will have a list of people to call, so you will be telling the truth when you say "...I have another call". And remember, if they want to order, TAKE IT!

Pat P, a Shaklee Sales Leader for 27 years, reports on the catalog orders that started coming in after she started using the catalog scripts:

"One week, I made 87 catalog calls. I left 47 messages, 7 called back, 4 placed orders. 3 will order next month.

"The next week I made more catalog calls and included people I hadn't spoken with and who hadn't ordered in years.

Spoke with 22 people and 8 placed orders.
2 will place orders next month.

"One person I called is an old customer
and only uses two products. She told me a
long time ago she didn't ever want anything
else. So, she hadn't gotten a catalog forever.
So after the class, I decided to send her a
catalog, even though I wondered if I'd be
wasting my time and my money. Then I left
her the 3 scripts message for the achy joint
product. Well, lo and behold, she called
back and ordered the pain product AND
said she wanted to put her husband on the
weight program…"

These and similar results from others in Study
Hall started the rumors about catalog empires in the
offing…

Referrals

A person you call who is not the one-in-ten will sometimes know someone who might be, and they may give you a referral on the spot.

Remember Sandra M of Shaklee who got two referrals from a cold lead? She said that "in ten years of doing the business, I have never gotten a referral from a stranger." Seven days since she started using her script, she got two, plus an order from the lead herself.

Patti K of Integris wrote me a note about several customers she had gotten using her script, including one who was now giving her referrals:

"One of the women who ordered last week is a preferred customer in North Carolina who has this month been responsible for $700 in orders. She called this morning with 5 more referrals. She's very busy and doesn't want to be a distributor…"

Here's how a conversation might go:

AUNT LULU

Well dear, that's not me. But I know someone who might want to know about a product like that. John Jones lives down the street. He has had [the problem you mentioned] and might want to know about it.

YOU

What's the best way for me to reach John Jones?

This way of asking the question puts the least pressure on Aunt Lulu regarding how she wants her friend John to be approached. You have given her the option of deciding. She can either give you John's number on the spot, or she can tell you that she will give John your number.

Treating people with respect this way increases the likelihood that they will listen again the next time you call and give you access.

Conversation with a Referral

You already know most of the script for this conversation. What's unique is just the opening, and three questions that position you as an advisor.

[Ring ring.]

YOU

Is this John Jones? …

This is Kim Klaver. **I'm calling you because Aunt Lulu said you might be able to answer a question for me. Do you have a minute?**

     REFERRAL

     Aunt Lulu, huh? OK. What's the question?

YOU

<u>My company's introducing</u> a product for people who…

     + Short First Date Script

And she said you might know someone who might like to know about a product like that? Is that right?

251

Since you don't know the person, your Short First Date Script may be more appropriate to use. However, if you have a relatively short First Date Script you can also go with the full Script.

REFERRAL

Yeah. She's probably talking about me. What have you got?

Here's where you ask 3 questions that position you as an Advisor. Ask them whenever someone asks you what you have and you don't know their situation.

For example, if you call Dell and tell them you are thinking of buying a computer, the sales person, who's trained to customize the system for you, will probably ask questions like: "What kind of computer do you have now? What do you want to use it for? What's important to you about a computer?"

We, too, customize what we offer the customer, and ask questions to enable us to do that. Here come the **3 Advisory Questions.**

YOU

I'm going to tell you what I've got here in just a second. Let me just ask you a couple of quick questions, may I?

[FBM   Pause]

> **[Q1.] What are you doing for (the situation) now?**
>
>> [Listen to the answer and acknowledge them in a neutral way. Even if you think they're doing something silly or that you disapprove of.]
>
> **[Q2.] How is that working for you?**
>
>> [Expect them to say, it worked for a while, but then it stopped working. Or it didn't really help much. For example, "It worked for a while then I fell off the wagon and I ate 5 boxes of chocolate truffles. When I get depressed I eat."]
>
> **[Q3.] How long has this been going on?**
>
>> Then, you do Scripts 2b and 2c in Chapter 9: "Let me tell you what happened to me…" ☺

Cold Market

I've always liked working the cold market because it's so big and there's no telling what I'll find. There are no friendships to ruin, and a 'No' from a stranger doesn't hurt as much as one from a friend.

Most cold market campaigns, however, either cost money, take time, or require 'nerve'. Take an inventory of your resources so that you can map out a cold market strategy that suits you. If you have lots of time and no money, don't pick a strategy that worked for someone with lots of money. If you'd rather not do business when you're running errands or at the gym, or if don't feel right about striking up conversations with strangers, put your foot down and don't do those methods. Even if people tell you it's easy. It may be easy for someone who feels different about those activities, but it won't be easy for you, and you'll end up not doing your business at all. If you have a budget to buy leads but have never done cold calls, practice a lot first, and start doing it with a buddy.

At the end of Part One, we talked about **Cold Cadaver Calling**. That is a cold market technique that costs nothing since you're calling out of the phone book or old leads lists you paid for some time ago. You're doing it **to practice your scripts** rather than to make sales. You know that the likelihood of finding a one-in-ten among cadavers is very small, so there's no undue disappointment when they say *No*. After making 100 cadaver calls with your First Date Script and 100 with your Short First Date Script, the scripts should be rolling off your tongue and you may be raring to take on real prospects.

You may want to start with your warm market, or by reviving old customers. If you've already done that, or if you choose not to go that route at all, then to the cold market we go to fill up your hot button club.

Here are three directions you can take in the cold market. You can do any or all of them, depending on your resources.

1.   Local businesses and neighborhoods

2.   Customer leads from brokers

3.   Bump-Intos

Ads are too complex to cover here. We also don't cover newsletters, talks, leads groups, trade shows, or flyers. If you have experience in any of these venues, try them. Use the Three Scripts formulas and principles and see what happens. We discuss these options in Study Halls and training calls as the need arises. Study Hall and call schedules are available at http://WhoWho911.com and are emailed to you when you sign up for the WhoWho911 newsletter.

Before you start any cold market campaign, have ready the material you'll be using to introduce yourself and what you're marketing – business cards or brochures with your personal contact information and Short First Date Script or byline, or a website that's free of seller talk or references to the business opportunity (see Chapters 20 and 21).

Local Businesses and Neighborhoods

Local businesses can be a fun source of regular customers and a source of steady orders. Knock on one door and you may get any number of customers or orders...

Which local businesses do you approach?

> Businesses you can visit personally, that are run by people who have the authority to buy. Not chain stores, because people who run them don't usually have buying authority.

> Businesses whose customers or clients are likely to be interested in YOUR fix. For example, if you're looking for people who want to lose weight and keep it off, you might target personal trainers, beauty salons, aestheticians, manicurists, and day spas. These folks have

clients who spend money to look better. This can be lots of fun if you enjoy talking to people.

How do you find them?

➢ Go through the Yellow Pages in your area – either the book or online -- and check out the businesses that appear to be owned by local business people. Select the upscale ones (whose customers can afford your products) and where the customers might want to know about your product.

➢ Online, http://superpages.com lets you search for businesses and individuals in any neighborhood in any area of the United States. http://whitepages.com and http://yellowpages.com are the online versions of the big phone books.

➢ If you don't know your neighborhood, do a drive–by to check out the businesses. Upscale beauty salons are good prospects if you have a weight script, and alternative physicians are good to try if you have a nutritional focus.

> Make a list of the businesses you've selected with their phone numbers and start by calling them on the phone...

What do you say? ...

Guess...

You're right. Same old same old... What's unique to this situation are the Openers and a few key phrases (underlined) interspersed through the conversation in between the scripts you know and love.

First Date Script when calling a local business:

[Ring ring]

YOU

(opener)

Hi. This is Lulu Sweet. This is __(name of the business you're calling) , right?

[*pause*]

OK. Good. I'm a local business owner[52] in town, and I'm calling every __(type of business), e.g. upscale hair salon to ask them a question. Do you have a second/minute?

---

[52] or 'merchant' or 'entrepreneur'

BUSINESS PERSON/RECEPTIONIST

OK. What's the question?

YOU

We're introducing a product for people who

> **+** Short First Date Script

Do you <u>have any customers/clients/patients</u> who
might like to know about a product like that?

[This is the end of the First Date part of the
conversation. Then come the 3 big questions,
remember?...]

BUSINESS PERSON/RECEPTIONIST

What is it?

YOU

+Script 1

+Script 2

So what do you think? Do you <u>*have any*</u>
<u>*customers/clients/patients*</u> who might like to
know about a product like that?

BUSINESS PERSON/RECEPTIONIST

Maybe. How does it work?

YOU

Do you have products that you market to your customers already?

BUSINESS PERSON/RECEPTIONIST

Yes.

YOU

Do you do it on a wholesale/retail basis?

BUSINESS PERSON/RECEPTIONIST

Yes.

YOU

This is like that. You get it wholesale and sell it retail.

[If there's interest]

Let me buy you a cup of coffee so I can show you what we've got and we can see if there's a match.

Tips When Talking to Local Business People

➤ Talk to the gatekeeper the same way as you would the owner. They have access to the owner, and might even be a relative. They often chat with clients, and they themselves may want your product. Make them feel special. You may be the only one who has made them feel special that day.

➤ Open by saying you're a business owner or merchant or entrepreneur in town because they're one also and it helps establish rapport.

➤ Second date. Have them try the product themselves.

➤ Tip re doctor's offices: Many doctors are not open to alternatives to drugs and don't want to take advice from someone who isn't also a medical doctor. When I marketed to MD's from my Yellow Pages, I looked for something in their ads that showed they were interested in alternatives – words like "prevention," "alternative medicine," "integrative clinic," "chelation," or "nutrition". A San Francisco medical doctor I found this way is still ordering boxes of the product I introduced him to ten years ago.

> If a local merchant falls in love with your product, they sometimes send out a personal endorsement letter to their customers, referring them to your product. Or they may ask you to do an in-office presentation for their clients. Often they will get a little percent from the sales generated. Sometimes they may become a distributor.

Neighborhood Door-to-Door. Instead of going to businesses, some people like canvassing their neighborhoods. Surprisingly many people enjoy this, especially in friendly, suburban neighborhoods. Stay close to home so you are in areas where you are familiar.

What do you say?

Here's an example of a neighborhood door-to-door First Date Script:

GREETING: **Hi. I'm Lulu Sweet your neighbor down the street.**

OPENER: **I'm calling on everyone in the neighborhood to ask a question. Do you have a second/minute? …**

SHORT FIRST DATE
SCRIPT: **My company's introducing a product for people who want a natural alternative to the hormone drugs they're taking like I did. Do you know anyone who might like to know about a product like that? …**

Formula: FDS for Neighborhood Door-to-Door

Hi. I'm (your name), your neighbor down the street. I'm calling on everyone in the neighborhood to ask a question. Do you have a second/minute?

+ Short First Date Script

If they say No, thank them for their time and say good-bye. If they say yes, proceed with Scripts 1, 2 and 3 in Chapter 9.

Here's an email that came in from Australia, from Rhonda B. whose husband went "door knocking" with his new First Date Script. He was inspired to go door-to-door after she had used her new script successfully with a bank teller. She wrote:

"Hi Kim! I sent you the story about the bank teller. After I told my husband about that he decided to make up his own script and off he went door-knocking (house to house) with one of our new "babies".

"They knocked on 54 doors, 24 were home. Out of the 24, 8 said no, 3 bought the starter pack on the spot and the rest are interested, to be followed up.

"They went out the next day and did one street only and sold one starter pack and signed a lady up who had watched them walk the whole street and was waiting her turn. She said she had been prospected before and was waiting for someone like us to come and sign her up…

"We have bought trainings from all the big trainers and we have seen nothing like what you have before. We feel hope now where there was lots of frustration for the last six years…"

- Rhonda B, Neways, Australia.

Customer Leads

Customer leads are names and contact data of people you don't know. You can get them from leads brokers who have gathered and organized consumers into categories of people who might be candidates for your club.

Where do you get customer leads?

1.   Local list brokers. Find them in your Yellow Pages. Brokers can give you leads classified in just about every category you can imagine – people interested in alternative health, self improvement, sports of all kinds, career-oriented, with or without children, retired, at a certain income level, living in a certain area, zip code, and on and on and on.

You can mail or call these leads using your Short First Date Script.

Talk to two or three list brokers, and tell them you're getting these lists because you're

---

introducing a product for people who...

+ Personal Market Segment.

Ask them to suggest some categories they have that include your personal market segment.

Always start small and local. Test 100 to 300 leads. Experiment until the leads category you come up with works with the First Date Script you have. Typical results are .5 to 3% response rate.

2. **Internet list brokers**. Some Three Scripts grads in my Study Halls have used http://www.usadata.com. You can ask for people in your own town, or any city, and narrow the selection by selecting several characteristics of the people you want. This company even provides postcards to do mailings directly from the site. You add your text, and they do the rest. There are various card designs to choose from. Most convenient. Leads prices depend on how many you get. For 300 leads with two classifications, e.g. self-improvement and alternative health, cost was about 17 cents per lead. Post cards and postage are extra.

Great way to practice doing cold market, given the low cost.

3. PM Marketing and Cutting Edge Media. PM Marketing at http://www.networkleads.com is another reliable source of customer leads. Peter Mingils, the owner, is a good friend and has been finding leads for direct sales and network marketing professionals for 10 years. We've used him extensively. Complete personal service included.

Cutting Edge Media at http://CEM.com is another well known leads service for our industry which we have used a lot.

4. For **additional lead sources**, go to Google.com and enter "mailing lists" and you'll see hundreds of them.

HINT: STAY LOCAL. It's much easier for you to talk to people who are interested, and perhaps meet them and get a group going. It's also much faster and less expensive. People who don't know you tend to prefer people who live close by when they're buying for the first time, especially the innovative kinds of products and services offered by direct sales and network marketing companies.

What do you say to customer leads?

First Date Script for Customer Leads

Sample Phone Conversation

GREETING: **Hi. I'm looking for Sandy Price. Is she there? This is Cheryl B. ...**

OPENER: **I'm calling you because I'm calling everyone in Luluville from this list that says that you're interested in self**

269

improvement and in health food. Is that right about you? ... Are you interested in self improvement and health food? ... I'm calling everyone on this list to ask a quick question. Do you have a minute?

SHORT FIRST DATE SCRIPT:

My company is introducing this product for people who take vitamins but are confused about which ones to take, like I used to be. Do you know anyone who might like to know about a product like that? ...

Formula – FDS for Customer Leads

Hi, I'm looking for (name of person on list*). Is she there? This is* (your name*).*

I'm calling you because I'm calling everyone in ___(area)___ from this list that says that you're interested in (description of the list characteristics*). Is that right about you?* ...

(OPTIONAL: *Are you interested in* (characteristics*) ? ...)*

Great. I'm calling everyone on this list to ask a question. Do you have a quick minute? ...

+ Short First Date Script

The Opener is the only piece that varies, depending on the type of lead you're using. All openers start and end with the same phrases. What varies are the characteristics of the lead list. Here are examples of different list characteristics. People who:

> ➢ responded to a health survey and said they had achy joints

> subscribe to Parent Magazine

> are interested in the environment, etc.

Here's what happened for Kay E of Shaklee when she tried the script.

"I was excited and wanted to try that new 3 Scripts script for cold calls. So I reviewed the script and started making the calls using the script... I got this woman who was interested. Then I used the packages script, just like you said, and she says "I like that, I like that" and then asked me, "What do you suggest? Where should I start?" I said just like you taught us, "Maybe start with the small one," and she said "Oh, that's just what I was thinking, I'd like to do that." I just felt so good when I put down that phone."

Bump-Into's

A Bump-Into[53] is someone with whom you have occasion to interact – even for just a few moments. The interaction gets to a point where they ask you: "What do you do?"

Remember that question? We spent most of Part One on how to answer it so that you don't get the glazed, change-the-channel-quick TiVo reaction -- the reaction many have reported getting in the past, causing them to conclude they don't know what to say. Many have confessed that they dread hearing the "What-do-you-do" question, even though it's what creates a selling opportunity.

Now, people who have their three scripts in hand say they can't wait to be asked. That's because they've had repeated good experiences when they use their script to answer the question. Here's

---

[53] Bump-Into's and scripts for recruiting are described in the Truth book, pp. 133-135

Kathy's Computer Store Story:

"The day after my 3-Script class I took my computer in and said I really needed it fixed, because I run my home business from the computer. The guy said, "So what do you do?" I remembered my script and said..."I market a product for someone who has had achy joints like I did..." He said: "My mother has arthritis, do you think it could help her??" I said "I don't know, but it worked for me..." He said: "Do you have a card?" WOW!! Short and simple--no seller talk, no promises, no generalities, no techno-babble (glyco's, phyto's, nutri's), no diseases...I was never sure just exactly what to say, NOW I DO!!"

- Kathy M, Mannatech Presidential

Bump-intos can be spontaneous, like Kathy's, or planned, like going to a Chamber of Commerce mixer. Everyone there knows they'll be trading the What-do-you-do question all evening, in the hopes of making a customer contact. Miriam G's story (Shaklee 10-year vet) illustrates this this:

"For years before I took the 3-Scripts course I always avoided going to any mixers, for fear someone would ask me what I did... Since the course, I am so prepared to answer the dreaded question, that when I went to a Chamber mixer last night I was what my sons would call a 'babe magnet.' I never have felt so attractive in my life, it felt GREAT... I had a steady stream of attracted people coming up to me the whole evening. Talk about having fun getting great leads... Thank you Kim for a class that has truly altered the course of my business. I've been doing it 10 years and now it's a whole new day."

Bump-intos can make standing in line lucrative. Why not pick up a customer at Kinko's, the Post Office, at the grocery store or at the airport…? Here's

Jean's Airport Story

"I was at the airport standing in the cattle stall C waiting to board Southwest Airlines when a gentleman came up to stand in line behind me. We struck up a conversation, and he asked me what I did. I used my script, and by the time I was finished, he asked me for my card, the man in back of him asked me for my card, plus the third man in back of him asked me for my card. He apologized for listening in on our conversation but said, I was describing him to a tee, and he wanted to learn more.

"Then, I sat down on the plane, and the man next to me struck up a conversation. When he got to the question what did I do, I once again used my script and by the time I was done he asked me for my card so he could share the information with his friends. When I asked him what he did he said, he was a salesman researching new opportunities. He gave me his card and asked me to call him in two weeks when he gets back from his vacation.

"It was so easy to do and so much fun to see people appreciate how important our product is to others. No more glassy eyed stares when I tell people what I do.

- Jean G, Ideal Health International

Small indulgence places are also good for finding the one-in-ten. Cappuccino or dessert houses, chocolate shoppes, day spas or tennis clubs. People always say they want to spend more of their time doing things they enjoy, like tennis, golf, hiking, sailing, spending a day at the spa or sipping a latte. Don't some of the products you market help people do those things as they age – without those achy joints, and without looking quite their age?

If you're someone who likes talking to people, doing bump-intos as a business strategy may suit you. If you are not one of those people (or at least not yet) – not to worry. Don't do it. Just remember to say your script when someone happens to ask you The Big Question. Some people are the strike-up-a-conversation type, some are not. If you aren't, best to do something else instead. ☺

Tips

When you find yourself in a bump-into situation, choose someone with whom to strike up a conversation – who is friendly-looking, and has good body language. You don't want to approach someone who is self-absorbed, or talking on a cell phone, or whose personality seems like an ingrown toenail.

The main scripts for bump-intos are the ones you memorized and practiced from Part One. Remember "I market a product for people who…" in response to "What do you do?" For bump-intos you'd use the short script with no zingers or results at the beginning. This is the cold market and you open the kimono even less than you do for warm market.

If someone asks you The Big Question spontaneously – without your having to set the stage for it, you're home free. You slide right into the scripts you've memorized and practiced.

If you want to make it happen, rather than wait for it to happen, you'll need to get good at striking up a conversation with a stranger. For example:

LATE NIGHT. KINKO'S

YOU
So, what are you doing here so late at night?

OR

Do you hang out/come here often?

> **THEM**
> Actually, I'm copying stuff for a talk I'm giving at my daughter's school.

YOU
Oh. So, what do you do during the day when you're not making copies? (haha)

THEM:
[whatever they do]

YOU
Neat. Do you love it?

THEM
[Usually they point out something they don't like

about what they do. Then, they might ask

The Big Q:]

What do YOU do?

Once they ask The Big Q, you've been asked out. It's your First Date! On the first cold market date, you do your Short First Date Script (rather than the full First Date Script), and if they show interest, you go right into the follow-up Scripts (See Chapter 9).

YOU:
[Short First Date Script]
Oh, I market a product for people who have achy knees when they go up and down the stairs, like what happened to me. Do you know anyone who might like to know about a product like that?

THEM
Yeah, maybe. What is it?

YOU

[Script 1]

It's a cream, a rub-a-dub that you put on your knees or any achy joints. That's what I did.

[FBM pause]

THEM
Oh yeah?

YOU

[Script 2c]

Actually, I liked the product so much I decided to go into business for myself and make it available to other people just like me. And that's what I'm doing…
etc. See Chapter 9.

Mary Jane M of Take Shake for Life thought up a unique way to combine bump-intos and handing out brochures. Here's how she did it.

Mary Jane's This-Is-Me Story

"I had my luggage checked on the plane so all I had in my hand was a purse and my brochures.... the brochures had my contact info, my before and after photo on it and my script... I spotted many extremely overweight people at the airport and I kept thinking to myself how do I get this information to them... I feel their pain and their shame, I know the consequences... so as I QUICKLY walked passed an overweight person, I handed them a brochure and I said, "THIS IS ME!!!" and walked away.

"I could see them out of the corner of my eyes. They looked at me, then looked at the brochure, and then looked back at me. The result was I handed out 10 to 12 brochures in two airports in two states. 8 people actually went to my website and signed up leaving me all of their contact information, and 4 people actually purchased products without even speaking to me..."

There are lots of ways to approach the great marketplace out there. Too many rely on seller talk and focus on closing the sale.

That way of approaching consumers may have worked once upon a time -- when national advertising had just come on the scene and consumers were not bombarded *ad nauseum* with sales pitches. Seller talk approaches don't work anymore. They turn people off. When people buy, they often do *despite* the pitches and the ads.

That's why we stay away from seller talk. (Notice that? hehe) The scripting formulas rely on your favorite fix, your hottest button. You tell your personal story, and ask if there's a match between consumer and story. That's all.

If not, next!

If yes, we proceed in the style of an advisor. We use language normal people understand to describe the product or service and its pricing. Then see what happens...

Messages

On Their Phone

*Y*es, it's good to leave a message. You might get a callback that will surprise you...

I've always left a message because it's a moment of time with someone. Our grads are reporting that they're getting callbacks now, whereas before they never did.

Bobbi R, a Shaklee rep, for example, had not called an acquaintance in the past, because she had worried that her friend's MD husband would want to know the science of the product. Armed with her new scripts, she finally called her friend. The woman wasn't home, so she left her Three Scripts message, like the one below.

Lo and behold, the next day, the woman called back and said, "That's something I would like to know about, and I have a couple of friends who'd like to know about it too. Let's get together…" [54]

The message scripts are very similar and sometimes identical, to the scripts for the actual conversations with people, from warm market to cold leads. What's unique to a message is the **"If End"**. Read the sample messages below and you'll see what I mean.

Sample Message for Someone You Know:

GREETING: **Hi Aunt Lulu. This is Mika.**

OPENER: **I'm calling everyone I know to ask them a question. Here goes.**

FIRST DATE SCRIPT[55]: **My company's introducing** a product for someone who has hit 50 and suddenly feels old, like what happened to me.

---

[54] In preparation for the meeting, Bobbi asked her friend whether her husband would want to know about the science behind the product. Her friend replied, "Oh, no, he won't want to know about that until after he knows it works for him. He doesn't care about the science of a product until he sees it works for him."

[55] Created in the Three Scripts class for Mika of Integris

You know that for most of my life I was pretty healthy and active. Then I turned 50, and suddenly I felt old. I was eating more junk food in the afternoon so I wouldn't fall asleep at my desk. I stopped exercising and put on 20 pounds... I tried about every new product in the health food store that might help, but nothing seemed to work.

Then one day I tried this other product, and within a month I noticed that I stopped conking out at my desk, and I didn't need junk food in the afternoon anymore... It's been 6 months now, and I can stay up the whole day without falling asleep. Suddenly, I don't feel old anymore.

Do you know anyone who might like to know about a product like that?

IF END: **If you do, give me a call.**

Here's my number.

000-000-0000.   I'll tell you what I've got and we can see if there's a match, OK? 'Bye.

Sample Message for Someone Who Responded to a Cold Call, Ad, Flyer, Postcard or other cold reaching out method:

GREETING: Hi. I'm looking for Harriet Cool. This is Lulu Sweet.

OPENER: I'm calling because you responded to an ad we ran.

PERSONAL MARKET

SEGMENT : for people who have achy knees when they walk up and down stairs. Does that sound like you?

IF END: **If yes, give me a call at 000-000-0000.**

I'll tell you what I've got and we can see if there's a match, OK? 'Bye.

Formula for Leaving Messages

Same script as for an actual first date conversation. End with:

If yes, give me a call at 000-000-0000. I'll tell you what I've got and we can see if there's a match, OK?   'Bye.

Memorize the 'If End' piece of the script If you decide to get your 100+ customers, you'll be using it a lot.

On Your Phone

To give the best impression:

1.   **Have a separate line or at least a separate voice mail box for your business.** You may even have more than one mail box for your business if you're running a marketing campaign. For example, if you're running an ad, you might dedicate one voice mailbox for ad responses:

"If you'd like to place an order, press 1.

If you're responding to the ad in the XYZ

Gazette, press 2. If you're looking for (your

name), press 3."

2.   **Instruct your kids <u>not</u> to pick up your business line.**

3.   **Do not record background music or family sounds** on your business message. Five kids singing and dogs barking may be endearing to friends and family, but it is not conducive to doing business.

4.   **When you record your message, stand up and smile.** Tense doesn't sell.   Friendly and

comfortable does. To make sure you have a little smile on, think of someone who really loves you, or someone you really love -- an animal, a child, your husband or wife, – or a peaceful or fun scene. So you don't sound like a seller but like an advisor or friend.

5.   **Hit pound immediately after you say "Here comes the beep."** (See script below.) That's to prevent a big pause between the end of your message and the beep. If there's a pause before the beep, some people start talking then and the beginning of their message is not recorded.

6.   **Listen to the message before it becomes permanent.** Listen with your consumer ears. Listen for sounds in the background, for hesitations, for the mood tone that comes through.   Listen that the beep comes right away after your message ends.   You may have to do 10 or 20 takes. It's worth it. Your message is the first impression your caller will get of you and your product or service.

Two Sample Messages for Your Answering Machine:

Sample Message #1

GREETING: **Hi, I'm glad you called.**

OPENER: **Let me tell you what we're doing**

FIRST SHORT DATE
SCRIPT[56]: **My company is introducing** a phone service for people who are tired of not knowing what their phone bill is going to be every month, like I used to feel. **Does that sound like you?**

CLOSE: If yes, leave your name and number and a couple of good times to reach you and I'll call you back. I'll tell you what we've got and we can see if there's a match. OK? Here comes the beep."

---

[56] Script from George L., Excel Communicatons

Sample Message #2

GREETING: **"Hi, I'm glad you called.**

OPENER: **Let me tell you what we're**
                             doing.

SCRIPT:

MARKET SEGMENT: **My company is introducing** a

product for people who worry

about having a heart attack, like I

used to. **Does that sound like**

you?

CLOSE: If so, leave your name and

number and a couple of good

times to reach you and I'll call you

back. I'll tell you what we've got

and we can see if there's a match.

OK?

"Here comes the beep."

Formula for Your Phone Message

Hi, I'm glad you called.
Let me tell you what we're doing.
My company is introducing[57] a product[58]
for someone[59] who...

+ Short First Date Script

If so, leave your name and number and
a couple of good times to reach you and
I'll call you back. I'll tell you what we've
got and we can see if there's a match.
OK? Here comes the beep.

---

[57] or "I'm introducing..."

[58] or "service"

[59] or "people" or "women" or "men" or "parents" or other appropriate group

Email Signatures

An email signature is a bit of text that appears at the bottom of an email. I have used it for years as a mini ad – a one- or two-line attention grabber, like a byline. Plus my name and contact information. Here's one:

> Kim Klaver
> I say no first
> http://whowho911.com
> 800-595-1956 • 816-454-1417

It doesn't cost anything, except the time it takes to create the text. I have 15 or 20 bylines which are set to rotate randomly. Once created, one keystroke causes one to appear at the bottom of each email I send.

Most people won't spend more than a few seconds reading text at the bottom of an email, so it needs to be short, with no seller talk whatsoever.

Something that causes someone to ask: "I wonder how she did that?" Or, "I wonder what he does?"

For example, here's a byline that Joan W., one of my Shaklee graduates, used:

"I don't get stomach aches anymore."

Here's what happened, according to Joan (9/4/03):

"I created a new signature byline in the Three Scripts class – at the bottom of my emails – and had almost forgotten about it this busy weekend when I received an email from my aunt in new York, responding to my byline about my stomach discomfort. She wanted to know how I had resolved it! I was a little shocked that she had bothered to comment on it because she has been very much against all the vitamins I take…"

The structure of her email appears below.

Hi Aunt Mary:

Blah blah blah blah blah. Blah blah blah blah blah blah blah. Blah blah blah blah blah. Blah blah blah blah blah blah blah blah blah blah blah blah. Blah blah blah blah blah blah blah…

Love,
Joan

I don't get stomach aches anymore.
www.mydomainname.com
000-000-0000

Using email signatures as a mini-ad is sometimes called "viral marketing". Sabeer Bhatia, co-founder of Hot Mail, created this technique to grow their subscriber base from zero to 6.5 million customers in its first 14 months, and was adding a stunning 40,000 members a day in 1996. He sold Hot Mail to Microsoft for a reported $400 million on December 31, 1997.

Now, other free email services also use viral marketing as a standard marketing tool. If you use one of those services, like Hot Mail or Yahoo, you may have noticed these mini-ads that appear automatically at the bottom of each email you send out. They advertise something that Hot Mail or Yahoo wants to put out there – often their free email service. And they always include a link the reader can click on to sign up.

You, too, can add your own mini-ad to your email. If you pay for your email service, nothing else appears at the bottom of your emails, and your own mini-ad will have the space exclusively. Otherwise, you share the space with Hot Mail or Yahoo, or other free email service.

Sample bylines

Here are some bylines I've created with my students in class. You can use them as models to create your own. The bylines use certain word structures and grammatical forms that put you in the consumer camp. Use them; otherwise, you risk falling into seller talk. See if you can pick out the structure and create one or more bylines for yourself.

- No more falling asleep at my desk for me.
- No more agonizing headaches for me.
- No more run-of-the-mill vitamins for me.
- No more acid throat for me and I did it without medication.
- No more choking down vitamin pills for me.
- No more achy joints for me. Without drugs.

- I can do 20 chin ups again.
- I can go skiing again.
- I can eat dairy again.
- I can get it up again.
- I can sleep through the night again.
- I can see my feet again. Without liposuction.
- I can wear my size 8 pants again, like before I had kids.
- I can wear my size 6 pants again, like before I turned 40.
- I can exercise like I used to.
- I can perform like I did when I was 30.

- Finally I can wear the same size I did before I had my baby.

- Now I can keep up with my grandkids.

- Now I can stay up until my teenagers come home.

- I don't need coffee to wake up in the morning anymore.

- I don't need Viagra® anymore.

- I don't need to sleep 10 hours a day anymore.

- I don't need 2 days to recover when I play basketball anymore.

- I don't have migraines anymore and I did it without drugs.

- I don't have to guess which vitamins to take anymore.

- I don't have to take 2 hour naps on the weekends anymore.

- I don't fall asleep reading to my kids anymore

- I don't fall asleep during the day anymore.

- I don't fall asleep unless I want to. Finally.

- ➢ I don't worry about high blood pressure anymore.
- ➢ I don't get clogged up anymore.
- ➢ I don't get a stuffy nose anymore.
- ➢ I don't sweat which vitamins to take anymore.

- ➢ My feet don't hurt when I walk anymore.
- ➢ My kids don't need their inhalers anymore.
- ➢ My headaches don't knock me out anymore.
- ➢ Headaches don't control my life anymore.

- ➢ I'm not worried about which vitamins to take anymore.
- ➢ I'm not taking two handfuls of vitamins anymore.
- ➢ I'm not jumping from one vitamin to another anymore.
- ➢ I'm not afraid anymore of dying too early, like my Mom did.
- ➢ I'm not cranky with my kids anymore.
- ➢ Now I'm not afraid I'm going to be sickly in my older years, like my Dad was.

- ➢ I thought I had lost my energy forever, but then I

> got it back.

> ➣ I now have energy to play with my kids.

> ➣ I have the energy to take my grandson fishing again. Finally.

> ➣ I have the energy to exercise again.

> ➣ I lost 65 pounds safely. Finally.

> ➣ I'm getting all my veggies without having to buy, chop or cook them.

> ➣ I laugh with my kids again.

> ➣ My skin looks like it did 10 years ago. Without surgery or drugs.

> ➣ Now I love walking my dog at 5:00 AM.

> ➣ I'm off the couch. I feel like I've got my future back.

> ➣ I found an alternative to Botox.

Most of my students' first attempts at a byline had some element of seller talk in it. It seemed like everyone went to the same school and learned how to create seller bylines. ☹

Here we're learning how to create **consumer** bylines, in the spirit of Ann Fudge's directive to the advertising world. To do that you state your 'name' –

your hot button, your favorite fix you experienced as a consumer when you first tried your product or service. . If someone is looking for your fix, or knows someone who is, they may reply to your email with an inquiry, or click on your website link. Just like they would if they were responding to an ad.

Common pitfalls

Some of the more common pitfalls in creating bylines are:

> **Preaching or proclamations:**
>
> Health and wealth for all
>
> Feel young again.
>
> Never be sick again.

> **Vague, general words:**
>
> Chasing away the signs of age.
>
> I have my energy back.
>
> I have my life back.
>
> I'm not overwhelmed anymore.

> **Extra words:**

I don't carry around all those 60 extra pounds anymore.

I have given up the guessing game of taking vitamins

> **Complicated or formal language:**

I'm not taking unmeasured vitamins anymore.

I no longer have signs of premature aging.

The flu passed me by.

> **Cutesy phrases:**

My get up and go got up and left.

I'm no longer sick and tired of being sick and tired..

My winter colds have flown south.

Now I leave my pain at the gym.

Checklist and 15 Tips

Here's a checklist of **7 questions to ask about your email byline** -- to make sure it is as effective as it can be. If the answer is YES to Questions 1 to 4, and NO to

Questions 5 to 7, you'll probably have a pretty good email byline.[60]

1. Is it about me or someone close to me?

2. Does it tell a little story about my favorite fix?

3. Are there picture words so that other people can "see" what I mean?

4. Is it language you'd use with a 13-year old?

5. Is it preaching or bossing?

6. Is it too cute?

7. Is there any seller talk (vague generalities, techno-babble, promises, chestbeating, screaming)?

Here are **15 tips for more effective email signatures**:

1. Get an email service that is not recognized as "free". Free services like Hot Mail or Yahoo give you small mailboxes which get full quickly

---

[60] If you want to make sure you have a good email signature, you can attend a Script Clinic. See the Three Scripts Resources page in the back of the book.

when you have a marketing campaign going. They give the impression that you're not a real business, since everyone knows they're free. Your ISP (Internet Service Provider whom you pay every month for internet connection) will usually have an email service or can give you recommendations on email providers. Earthlink, SBC Global, Comcast, Onebox, and AOL are some of the more popular ones.

2.   **Include a link to your website, if you have a customer-friendly website.** (See the next item below to determine whether you have a usable website.) The link includes the entire address of the website, e.g.: http://whowho911.com. That will allow the reader to click on it right from your email.

3.   **Do NOT use a web site that:**

a.   **Talks about the business.** Business talk tends to disappoint or scare away a consumer who is simply interested buying a product, not doing a business. Remember, 97-98 percent of people are customers, not sellers, of the products they use. Don't you want to connect with them?

b. **Is hypey or filled with techno-babble**. This is seller talk, which turns off most consumers. Better not to mention a website at all than use one that turns off an interested person. They can always hit "Reply" to your email to contact you. Much safer. This may mean saving your company website for existing distributors, or people looking into the business. Not for first-date customers.

4. Make sure that the link goes directly to the page describing the product to which your email signature refers. NOT to the company home page, or to a page that describes other products. Why make the consumers hunt for the product they're interested in? Most won't take the time, would you?

5. **You can get your own domain name** and have it forward to the page you want. Your domain name itself can be a marketing tool. For example, http://www.ImNotPoopedOutAnymore.com. You can buy domain names from Network Solutions.com or GoDaddy.com or many other domain name services and have it forward to the exact web page you choose.

6. **Test your email signature before
using it** by sending yourself an email with the signature.
See how it looks. Test the link if you have one and see
how it looks from the perspective of the reader.

7. **Set your email signature so that one
appears automatically on EVERY email you send
out**, including personal correspondence. You're not
mounting a specific marketing campaign. You're simply
taking advantage of emails you're already sending out to
tell your mini-story to more people. The Help menu in
your email program will give you instructions on how to
set your email signature.

8. **Check for spelling errors.**

9. **No screaming**: No bold or colored
type. No capital letters except at the beginning of a
sentence or for proper names. No exclamation points.

10. **No preaching**. "Health and wellness for
all!" or "Get rid of your problems." or "Change your
life." or even "Do you want to look younger?" Instead,
describe a fix that happened to you. Just like saying "I'm
a redhead now, finally." Who does that call to?

11.   **Do NOT ADD the obvious seller question**: "What about you?" OR "Do you want that, too?" Allow the reader the pleasure of going: "Ah, yes, that sounds like me."

12.   **Do not include the name of your product or company.** That, too, is seller talk. Here's an example of this problem from a student who had created a good byline, then added a second line with seller talk:

> Name
> No more achy joints for us...
> Thanks to Company X's great new Pain
> Management Products! (☹)
> name@domainname.net
> 1-888-000-0000

It's a much more intriguing email signature without the third line. Agree?

13.   **You can use an 800 number, but also include a local number** so that people know you're local and real. Especially for local cold market campaigns.

14. **Create several email bylines** for your different fixes, and set your email program so that they are randomly selected. You can always manually override the random selection.

15. **You can use your email byline on your business card, on labels that you put on brochures, yellow page ads, postcards and other direct mail pieces.**

Sample email signature:

Lulu Paws
No more achy joints for me. Without drugs.
http://www.YourDomainName.com
800-000-0000 • 212-000-0000

A Website for Customers

Most companies have websites which describe their business opportunity and the product line. Company reps can get usually get their own personalized company site, called a "self-replicating website". Every distributor's site looks the same except for the personal info – a picture and a short bio of the distributor. A customer can place an order on the site, and it is credited to the distributor.

These company sites are not designed to be first date sites for new customer (or business) prospects. Instead, they're designed to educate the reps and show new products, services or twists in the pay plan, or announce company trainings or events Rarely has someone reported that they got an order from of these sites.

All 200+ company sites I've reviewed, mix in their products with offers to earn income with the business opportunity. That's when I decided it was time to create a *first date* customer site for my Three Scripts grads. A place for a marketer to send customer prospects, that would be based on their hot button "fixes", one at a time without confusing or putting off a potential customer with the business opportunity.

The site, http://alternativenetworkmarketing.com has two separate entrances. One for someone who's looking for a business of their own, and another for someone who's looking for an alternative fix to a problem or situation they're experiencing. They are totally separate.

Say you want to show someone what you market online. You give them a web address and they can go look whenever they want – 24/7 around the world. Your personal First Date Script is printed right on the site, for the world to see. One can have a page for each fix that is being offered – "for someone who…"

To see an example of one of these web pages, "for someone who has achy knees when they go up and down stairs, like I used to…"go here:

http://anmnow.com/anm/company.shtml To see an example of a phone service for people who… being introduced, check this DEMO page http://anmnow.com/images/site_images/productpage.html

   If you are interested in one of these sites, go to the bottom of either of the above pages for sign up info. There are recorded audios right online for you to hear the latest conference calls on the system. At http://www.alternativenetworkmarketing.com/ half way down the page you will see the "Audio" link.

   This way, anyone who wants to show consumers what they have online can do so and stay in the FDS language mode. And of course, NO ONE sees anything about the business – anymore than you'd expect to see a pitch on how to make money selling cable TV on your cable TV web page.

   ANM is a growing online community of like-minded people who want to focus on customer gathering, and keep the business opportunity separate.

Members get regular tips and training calls on getting traffic to their site.

Here's what's been happening:

Deb B, of Ideal Health reports:

"I've had my site with Kim for two months. I'm new at this too and I've learned a lot - and I've already put in 6 new customers with this site - and they were national. I never would have gotten them from my warm market. Just from sending them to my customer site. And I just started sending them 3 weeks ago...

And here's an email from Brenda C:

Hi Kim: I just HAVE to tell you what happened today. I took the 3 scripts class last weekend, and on Monday I changed my website so it would say what I learned it should say. Today (Wednesday) I got a preferred customer! She came to my site from a pay per click. She read the script- and signed herself up! This is amazing! … Thank you so much for teaching something that really works!! No more 3 PM slump for me!!"

Next...

I have proposed an approach in this book that is probably heresy for most people in network marketing today. The most controversial points of the approach are: the initial focus on getting regular customers instead of business builders,[61] not mentioning the product or company name or other techno-babble on the "first date" with a prospect, accepting that your thing is not for everyone, leading with your own hot button instead of probing for theirs, and sticking with that focus until you get your 100 loyal customers. It's NOT easy. No product sells itself. One must practice, practice, practice.

This is the opposite of what has been taught for decades. So the question is, should you go this route or not?

---

[61] Of course you don't turn away people who want to join your business; you just don't actively pursue them in the beginning

Here's how to decide: Is what you're doing now working for you or not? Are you happy doing what you're doing in the business or not? Are you proud of it? Do the things you do give you inner satisfaction or not? Are they "you" or not? Do you love it madly or not?

If yes, keep doing what you're doing. And pass this book on to someone who has lost faith in themselves and the business.

If your answer is 'No', I offer you my hand to lead you along the less traveled road. I offer you the stories that my graduates have told at Study Halls, and in public conference calls. Some are in this book, others on the website, and they keep coming in.

Finally, I offer you the success of American companies like AOL and the cable TV industry to demonstrate that setting up a loyal customer base is a good and profitable foundation for your business.

There will be obstacles to overcome, distractions to set aside, and pressures to deal with. Your sponsor and other upline may belittle and ridicule your new approach. They may pressure you into going back to pursuing only business builders – those 1 in 1,000 or 10,000 – and ignore the customers, who number more like 1 in 10. Or they may ignore your strength and insist you do **their** reaching out method which is not you. Or your company will tempt you with new products which don't relate to your hot button. Or someone may offer you the opportunity to sell to an audience that is not related to your hot button. Or you may hear a success story from someone who is doing something different – something you don't connect with, but which now distracts you.

But I say to you: Do not falter. Do not give in. Do not give up on **your** hot button club. Remember this: 95% of those doing the business the old way drop out, discouraged and upset. Second, 97-100% of the income that companies with a real product or service get, comes from people ordering the products and services each month. That includes many inactive distributors. Only 3% of a network marketing company's customers also sell the products regularly.

Where but in our industry have customers gone out of vogue? But it's hard to teach old dogs new tricks. The old dogs "laughed in 2001 when Steve Jobs introduced the iPod, Apple's $400 MP3 player. They laughed in 2003 when he opened the iTunes Music Store, selling songs for 99 cents when millions of consumers were downloading tracks for free. But Jobs is having the last laugh...having sold 5 million iPods. Apple owns 55 percent of the music player market..." (*Wired* magazine, 6/04, p 107)

Seth Godin weighs in with his take on the role of customers in the title of an article in Fast Company, "Contempt of Consumer: It's a Real Crime."

I offer you Einstein's advice:

"The significant problems we face cannot be solved at the same level of thinking we were at when we created them."[62]

---

[62] http://www.jokemonster.com/quotes/quotes/a/q130982.html

Q & A

These are the questions that have often come up in Study Halls or at the end of a Three Scripts class. One or two may have popped up for you too...

Question 1. When we use just our First Date Script, or Market Segment Script aren't we excluding others who might want something different?

Yes, you are intentionally excluding people who belong to a market segment that is different from yours. You are not calling their name. On a "first date", the most effective way to make sure that people who are ready to buy will hear their name is to call ONE NAME AT A TIME. If you call more than one name at a time (i.e. talk about all your products), you may lose the one who is ready to buy from you.

If you start listing everything you have in the hopes that there will be a match, you lose the person's attention. On a FIRST DATE no one cares enough to hear about all the products you have. What gets someone's attention is hearing about something specific, something that touches them, either for themselves or someone they know.

Exclusivity is an aphrodisiac, at least in this culture. When someone says you can't have something, do you want it more or less? Think about your children... It's the forbidden fruit syndrome.

Offering ONE FIX AT A TIME has a surprise bonus: referrals, referrals, referrals. Students in Three Scripts classes and Study Halls have reported unprecedented increases in referrals, both from people they know and people they don't know. One woman reported that she got 16 referrals in one week, more than she had had in her entire 12-year career.

P.S. Letting go of "the others" might be easier if you think of it like shopping for shoes. Say you go downtown to buy a pair of women's running shoes. With that one decision, you have just excluded ALL the hundreds of men's shoes. And, when you look for your running shoes, you have just now also excluded every other kind of women's shoe they have in the store. But you nose around, try on different types of running shoes, and eventually you find the right pair. Now you have what YOU want – a match for what you were looking for, yes?

When you take your new running shoes home, do you think about the thousands of shoes you left in the store? Do you pine for all those other shoes? Or are you happily looking forward to wearing your ONE PAIR of new shoes?

Question 2. Should I play to the person to whom I'm speaking? You know, try other "for people who" stories even if they aren't mine, if it seems like they want another product?

Generally, the answer is NO. Stick to your knitting.

First, using YOUR first date script over and over and over and over and over and over and over ensures that it will roll off your tongue in a natural and effective way night or day, drunk or sober. And often if the person you're talking to isn't in the market for your fix, but has a friend who is, they will hear their friend's name, and give you a referral.

Second, you'll get skill and confidence you didn't have before, so that you can specialize, like doctors do. Why not become the person in your area who is KNOWN as that person who has a product, say, "for people who have aches and pains and don't want to use drugs to get rid of them?" Or "who want to reduce those lines without Botox"? What if you become like the cardiologist everyone knows, who specializes in heart conditions? Or the foot specialist or eye specialist?

If you want, after you get those first 100+ customers using your first date script, you can do another first date script for another fix that has meant a lot to you. But do ONE at a time. So people begin to perceive you as the person who has a product for people who…

Third, the market segments my students have described and of which they are a part, all include tens of millions of people. Finding 100 customers in 100 days is not a question of market size, but how often you will offer your first date script so those out there will hear their name being called.   Why not go for 1000 customers in 1000 days going after the SAME market segment? Isn't this working smarter instead of harder?

One lady reported that she was offering a product "for moms of children who were picky eaters and worried their children weren't getting the right nutrition". She said that after the one mom bought the product for her child, she was invited by that mom to several group meetings of other moms to make her presentation – one at a day care center where she'd met the first mom, and another home-schooling group in the neighborhood.

This happens when you can show you are a knowledgeable member of the market segment you are calling for.   It makes it easier for people to identify your specialty and pass it on. Rather than showing up as a Jack-of-all-trades and master of none. Or worse, being perceived as just another seller bear.

IF MY PRODUCT'S SO HOT, HOW COME I CAN'T SELL IT?

Fourth, the learning curve is MUCH quicker when you repeat the same script more often, over a shorter period of time.   Dr. Gawande reports on a Harvard Business school research group that studied learning curves among surgeons. They followed 18 cardiac surgeons and their teams "as they took on the new technique of minimal invasive cardiac surgery…The new heart operation…proved substantially more difficult than the conventional one… All teams received the same three-day training session and came from highly respected institutions with experience in adopting innovations. Yet, in the course of fifty cases, some teams managed to halve their operating time while others failed to improve at all…

"One physician made several visits to observe one of the quickest-learning teams and one of the slowest, and he was startled by [what he found]… The surgeon on the fast-learning team was actually quite inexperienced compared with the one on the slow-learning team—he was only a couple of years out of training. But he made sure to pick team members with whom he had worked well before and to keep them together through the first fifteen cases before allowing any new members. He had the team go through a dry run before the first case, then <u>deliberately scheduled six operations in the first week, so little would be forgotten in between</u>. He convened the team before each case to discuss it in detail and afterward to debrief. He made sure results were tracked carefully…"

This is precisely what we teach in the Three Scripts class and in Study Hall. Find a buddy to do the calls with, practice the calls first, then do a whole bunch of them one right after another, with discussion after each call to help improve the next one. The same first date script is used each time. We have everyone do 100 calls minimum the first week, since the calls last less than 5 minutes in most cases. The results have been a renewed motivation and significant increases in sales.

I rest my case.

Question 3.   I've heard some people made it really fast.   So did they have to practice this much?

When I first got involved in the business, the two stories I heard most were about the wild success of 1) a former tuna boat fisherman, now a top earner, who says he knew nothing about anything, and who laughed about not even being able to figure out his paycheck, and 2) a former waiter, who had sponsored the tuna boat fisherman, who had suddenly become the #1 big banana in the company.

Both stories, while encouraging to all, were not what they seemed at first blush, and I have found this to be true for nearly every single top person I know across nearly 100 companies today.

Both young men above worked round the clock in their network marketing businesses. However, both also had years of network marketing experience before they got involved with their then current company, which I was with, also. The top earner in the company had been raised in a network marketing family, and his father had had a heart attack in his 40s, due to the stresses related to his network marketing business. So the son had grown up with the business, and had had years of experience before joining the current company. And he recruited many of the people that had been part of the previous company.

The point is, that none of this was ever discussed. Nothing false was stated. The whole story was just never presented. So people got the impression that you could step off a tuna boat and make a million dollars a year within a year. Or that a simple waiter could earn twice that within a year or two. Both were true, but there were YEARS of experience before that which undoubtedly helped them.

This is true for countless leaders in today's companies. Many have 20+ years experience before they strike it rich, but no one mentions those prior years. What you hear is just that in this particular company, in three to four years, or less, they're now earning $10k+ per month.

What's good, I suppose, is that that attracts people. What's bad is that many people feel like failures if they don't succeed BIG within 10 or 12 months. Many quit if they're not earning fat incomes within a year, like the "big boys" said they did.

So when you hear the big stories, ask what else that person has done in their past. That might help explain their current success. Peter Drucker, America's #1 management expert, says:

> "For the first four years, no new enterprise produces profits. Even Mozart didn't start writing music until he was four."

Give yourself that much time to replace your current income, or to earn the average income in the US today, which is a bit less than $3k per month.

Question 4. If you were so successful bringing in the business builders, why are you changing strategy now and teaching people to go after customers?[63]
Several reasons.

First, I don't know if I could duplicate in the current marketplace what I did years ago. There are too

---

[63] John Fogg asked this question during an interview on his weekly call for network marketers 12.23.03.

many dead bodies of failed aspiring business builders around today. Almost everyone out there knows someone who tried and didn't make it, so they run the other way when they see the circles on the wall. It's becoming more and more difficult to find good leads, people willing to try.

I am no longer optimistic that it's possible to reverse the extremely high drop out rate of entrepreneurs in network marketing, with the old methods of going after business builders. I used to think I could do that by teaching people all the survival skills I had learned in building my own organization. But even with those skills, there are too few Aces out there to meet the demand. Finding an Ace today is almost like winning the lottery.

I realize now that most people I thought were business builders, were really one-shot high volume customers. We called them "turbos". They bought a large initial order (US$2-5,000, sometimes even $25,000) because they loved the product a lot and thought it would sell itself. But many of them found out they weren't cut out for the direct sales world. So they ended up dropping out or just buying the product for their personal use.

The turbos were the monthly extra shots in the arm, but I had to prime the pump each month to get those shots the next month. That was not sustainable for most people. What saved us all were the regular product users – the "lovers" -- who loved the product and took it each month. I still take it today and buy it for members of my family, even though I have long since passed my business back to the company.

I've always had a healthy respect for "lovers" because there were so many of them, and together they contributed significantly to my income every month. So I set up an automatic reorder program within the company to make it easier for the lovers to get the product and, if they were so inclined, to sell it to other lovers. I realized already then that the steady income from lovers comprised insurance against months when no builders were to be found.

What has distressed me so much over the past few years is how many people come to me because they've been told that getting customers is not important. That there's no money in anything but recruiting. This means that the lovers are being shown the door. Suddenly, those who love the product and like to find others like that don't matter anymore. This is NOT a good thing. Without regular loyal customers, can there be a company that is built to last? Where but in our industry have customers gone out of vogue?

I have discovered that my numbers are pretty industry-standard. In my business years ago, perhaps two to three percent of all those who took the product each month were people who also sold it to others and perhaps found another builder. That has turned out to be the case for the major companies and the top distributors I have worked with – companies that have a real product or service that is good enough such that people would use it even if they weren't selling it. Like Shaklee, Mannatech, Ideal Health, Melaleuca, Excel Communications, NuSkin, Arbonne, Life Force, Tahitian

Noni, Seasilver, and many others. Of all their regular customers, only two to three percent also do the business.

Second, as I was moping about wondering what I could do about the decline in network marketing for my students and my online monthly newsletter subscribers, I began noticing the write-ups Dell Computers was getting almost each quarter. Dell had become Number One in PC sales, and still is Number One, beating out IBM, and the combo of HP and Compaq.

Every write-up and financial analysis I saw stated that the reason Dell was Number One was their marketing method: DIRECT SALES. In describing Dell's quarterly earnings report posted 5.16.02, the New York Times reported that "Dell is gaining market share during the industry's difficult times…The Dell advantage lies not in technology, since all the largest PC makers rely on Intel's microprocessors and Microsoft's Windows operating systems. But Dell has perfected its direct-marketing model of selling to companies and consumers

Q & A

over the Internet or telephone, without resellers or
retailers…" Dell's company reported "revenue of more
than $8 billion in the quarter." [64]

Clearly, the marketing method we're all using –
going directly to customers is the right thing to do. Look
at Dell's results! So I created the "Dell Advantage"
classes a few years ago, to teach people how to get
customers through the direct sales techniques that had
worked for me.[65]

At about that time, I noticed the big hoopla
surrounding the merger of AOL and Time Warner. I
was astounded when the new company was named AOL
Time Warner. AOL got first place in the name even
though they were a much younger company. Analysts
said it was AOL's 30 million monthly customers that
gave them that kind of clout.

Our profession has both what Dell has -- the
direct sales approach -- and what AOL has -- monthly

---

[64] Steve Lohr (May 2002), *The New York Times*. P. C5
[65] Paula English taught parts of that class with me.

customers. So, why not combine those winning features when describing and doing network marketing?

Last, I have been following the news about cable TV, having been a closet movie and TV producer type for years now. And guess what analysts mention most often about the cable TV business model? … That's right, it's their monthly customer/subscriber base. According to a recent report both by Fox News and the *New York Times*, there are some 62 million households that subscribe to cable TV, paying an average of $55 per month. This is their edge. Each month that income comes in. Note that both AOL and cable TV do this with NO downline. So, why not focus on this part of our business?

Aren't direct sales and network marketing companies like AOL and cable TV because they have products and services people buy one time from a rep and then can re-order on their own in an auto-ship arrangement? And we do direct sales like Dell, don't we?

These observations were the inspiration behind the *Do You Have a Plan B?* book and the "Three-Scripts

100 customers 100 days" classes. Why not focus on the monthly customers, like cable TV and AOL have done? Why not have insurance income while waiting for that elusive business builder to show up?

How much would you earn if you had 100 customers who buy what you do every month? What about 1,000 monthly customers? ...

And there you have it...

References

American Heritage Dictionary of the English Language. 2000. New York: Houghton Mifflin.

Gawande, Atul. 2002. *Complications: A Surgeon's Notes on an Imperfect Science.* New York: Picador, Henry Holt.

Godin, Seth 2004. "Contempt of Consumer: It's a Real Crime," *Fast Company*, September.

Godin, Seth. 2003. *Purple Cow.* New York: Portfolio, Penguin.

Klaver, Kim. 2002. *Do You Have a Plan B?* Kansas City, MO: Max Out Productions.

_____. 2001. *Rules for the New New MLMer.* Kansas City, MO: Max Out Productions.

_____. 1996. *So You Want to Be a Networker* (audiotape). Kansas City, MO: Max Out Productions.

_____. 1997. *How to Build a Giant Heap without Your Friends, Family, or Neighbors* (audiotape). Kansas City, MO: Max Out Productions.

Lohr, Steve. 2002. *The New York Times*, May, p. C5.

Ruiz, Don Miguel. 1997. *The Four Agreements.* San Rafael CA: Amber Allen Publishing.

Strunk, William Jr. and White, E.B. 2000. *Elements of Style, Fourth Edition.* Boston: Allyn and Bacon.

Taub, Erica. 2004. "How Do I Love Thee TiVo?", in *New York Times*, "Circuits," March 18.

Tharp, Twyla. 2003. *The Creative Habit*. New York: Simon & Schuster.

Wired Magazine. 2004

Three Scripts Resources

1. **Single and bulk orders of this book**
   are available at
   http://www.whowho911.com/paperback.html

2. **Three Scripts Classes and Three Scripts Stud
   Halls** Information, reviews and schedules:

   http://www.whowho911.com/3scripts2.html

   **Companies or distributors who would like to set
   company-specific classes may contact Kim Klave**
   kim@whowho911.com.

3. **To Catch A Mini-Ace Class Schedule** (for
   Three Scripts grads only)
   http://www.whowho911.com/ace.html

Annotated Works
by Kim Klaver (aka Ms. Stud)

Books

Do You Have a Plan B? For entrepreneurs who are looking to supplement or replace their JOB or current business. This book shows how direct sales and network marketing are similar to mainstream business models of Dell, AOL, cable TV, Amazon and McDonald's.

Rules for the New New MLMer. For networkers who want to avoid 'the 5 worst things to say to a good prospect' and learn new ways to approach them. Plus how to say "No" first and preserve one's self esteem, and tips on Internet marketing.

The Truth. What It Really Takes to Make It in Network Marketing. A 200-page full color cartoon book for network marketers who are looking for real-life demonstrations of 14 recruiting methods, team dynamics and business survival skills .

Audios – available in a package or singly

So You Want to Be a Networker? Audio tape with skits and sound effects to introduce prospects to network marketing. Reminds networkers about what it takes to make it in this business

How to Build a Giant Heap with or Without Your Friends, Family Or Neighbors. 2-tape set for networkers who want to learn recruiting methods where people come to you, and how to respond to tough questions, including "Is this a pyramid?" "How much do you earn?" and more.

How to Be an Awesome Sponsor and Keep Your Heap. Audio tape showing how to keep your team together and create a mastermind program to overcome obstacles that knock people out of the business. Tips from Napoleon Hill and Jesus.

Survival Skills For the Advanced Heap Builder. Audio tape for networkers who want to attract people who already have other income streams. Shows how to present a network marketing business as an "income producing asset" a la Robert Kiyosaki.

Websites
http://www.maxout.com or
http://www.WhoWho911.com

All books, tapes and classes available at:
http://www.WhoWho911.com
http://www.WhoWho911.com/store.html
800.595.1956 or **816-454-1417**

About the Author

Kim Klaver, aka Ms. Stud has been a marketing renegade ever since she can remember. She put out her first industry-wide audiotape *So You Want to Be a Networker?* in 1996. Her radical approaches to marketing are all based on an uncanny understanding of how to open people's minds, a masterful use of language, and doing it since she was eight.

In her first attempt as a professional direct seller, Kim retailed more water filtration units than anyone in the company's history -- nearly $60k in her first month alone. Five years later, when she found another product she loved that people bought month after month after month, Kim built an organization of 31,000 people in 13 months, and made it to the highest possible position in the shortest time in company history.
(http://whowho911.com/aboutus.html)

In 1996, responding to the thousands of requests to put her attitude and tips on tape and make her fun techniques available to anyone looking for alternatives to the status quo, Kim gave up her interest in specific networking companies, and founded Max Out Productions. Now she shares her secrets and insights with the entire industry through her books, tapes, website and classes.

She is the mastermind behind the biggest network marketing website on the net, http://whowho911.com . The website now gets 5 million hits a month and has been featured in countless magazines, websites and newsletters.

Kim's masterful use of language began at MIT in 1970 where she nearly failed "the" introductory linguistics class taught by the world renowned Noam Chomsky. So she wrote *From Deep to Surface Structure* that summer, published by Harper & Row, NY in 1971. It became the basic textbook for the introductory linguistics course at MIT and other universities across the U.S. The foreword was written by Noam Chomsky.

At Harvard in 1972 she wrote language tests for children. The *Bilingual Syntax Measure* was published in 1972 and 1973 by Harcourt Brace, NY. These cartoon style tests are used in elementary schools throughout the US. During that time she earned a Master of Arts in Teaching degree from Harvard.

She continues to write, teach, and lead the alternative network marketing movement from her home in Mill Valley, California, online and on the phone around the world. More about Kim at http://whowho911.com/aboutus.html.

Heidi Dulay has co-authored or collaborated with Kim on five previous books, and in building her largest network organization. She is writing a book on her new Food Cycling Program for people who can't

keep weight off. She is a certified nutritionist and
hypnotherapist, holds a doctorate from Harvard in
human development, and teaches Tibetan qigong. More
about Heidi at http://www.littlespa.com/about.html

"Kim delivers eloquently with great brilliance, wisdom and panache while making a "heap of their own" a reality for thousands of aspiring networkers around the globe."

-Mark Victor Hansen
Co-Author, Chicken Soup for the Soul ©

Dear Kim: Congratulations on becoming the first NSA distributor in its 25-year history to go directly to the Executive Presidents' Advisory Council in your first year as National Marketing Director (the top position possible in NSA).

-John J. Blair
VP, Sales & Marketing, NSA
July 24, 1995